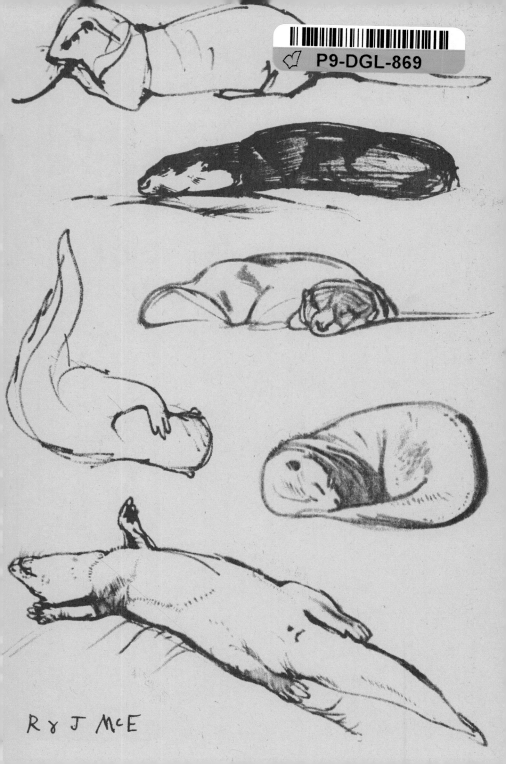

R y J McE

Ring of Bright Water

by Gavin Maxwell

HARPOON VENTURE
BANDIT
PEOPLE OF THE REEDS
THE TEN PAINS OF DEATH
RING OF BRIGHT WATER

RING
OF BRIGHT
WATER

Gavin Maxwell

NEW YORK
E. P. Dutton & Co., Inc.

First published in the U.S.A. by E. P. Dutton & Co., Inc., 1961
Copyright, ©, 1960 by Gavin Maxwell
All rights reserved. Printed in the U.S.A.

EIGHTH PRINTING MAY 1961

LIBRARY OF CONGRESS CATALOG CARD NUMBER: 61-5998

For John Donald
and Mary MacLeod of Tormor

He has married me with a ring, a ring of bright water
Whose ripples travel from the heart of the sea,
He has married me with a ring of light, the glitter
Broadcast on the swift river.
He has married me with the sun's circle
Too dazzling to see, traced in summer sky.
He has crowned me with the wreath of white cloud
That gathers on the snowy summit of the mountain,
Ringed me round with the world-circling wind,
Bound me to the whirlwind's centre.
He has married me with the orbit of the moon
And with the boundless circle of stars,
With the orbits that measure years, months, days, and nights,
Set the tides flowing,
Command the winds to travel or be at rest.

At the ring's centre,
Spirit, or angel troubling the pool,
Causality not in nature,
Finger's touch that summons at a point, a moment
Stars and planets, life and light
Or gathers cloud about an apex of cold,
Transcendent touch of love summons my world into being.

Foreword

IN WRITING THIS book about my home I have not given to the
house its true name. This is from no desire to create mystery—
indeed it will be easy enough for the curious to discover where I
live—but because identification in print would seem in some
sense a sacrifice, a betrayal of its remoteness and isolation, as if by
doing so I were to bring nearer its enemies of industry and urban
life. Camusfeàrna, I have called it, the Bay of the Alders, from the
trees that grow along the burn side; but the name is of little consequence, for such bays and houses, empty and long disused, are
scattered throughout the wild sea lochs of the Western Highlands
and the Hebrides, and in the description of one the reader may
perhaps find the likeness of others of which he has himself been
fond, for these places are symbols. Symbols, for me and for many,
of freedom, whether it be from the prison of over-dense com-
munities and the close confines of human relationships, from the
less complex incarceration of office walls and hours, or simply
freedom from the prison of adult life and an escape into the forgotten world of childhood, of the individual or the race. For I am
convinced that man has suffered in his separation from the soil
and from the other living creatures of the world; the evolution
of his intellect has outrun his needs as an animal, and as yet he must
still, for security, look long at some portion of the earth as it was
before he tampered with it.

This book, then, is about my life in a lonely cottage on the north-
west coast of Scotland, about animals that have shared it with me,
and about others who are my only immediate neighbours in a
landscape of rock and sea.

Camusfeàrna   GAVIN MAXWELL
October 1959

Acknowledgements

WE ARE INDEBTED to the following for permission to quote copyright material:

Messrs. Faber and Faber Ltd for 'Thank You' from *The Earth Compels* by Louis MacNeice; Miss Kathleen Raine and Messrs. Hamish Hamilton Ltd for 'The Ring' from *Year One* from which the title of this book is taken; and the literary agents of the late Mr Ernest Thompson Seton for an extract from *Life Histories of Northern Animals*, published by Messrs. Constable and Co. Ltd.

The drawings on pages 108 and 109 are by Michael Ayrton.

The untitled drawings in the text are by Peter Scott, except for those on pp. 11 and 36 by Robin McEwen, and on pp. 23 and 66 by the author. The end-papers are by Robin and John Sebastian McEwen.

All photographs are by the author, with the exception of the panorama of Camusfeàrna, by Robin McEwen.

List of Illustrations

A lost marble
Asleep before the gas fire in London
Relaxing from play
An eye on the photographer
Rubber fruit that squeaked were among Mij's favourite toys
Lutrogale perspicillata maxwelli

PART I

The Bay of the Alders

1

I sit in a pitch-pine panelled kitchen-living room, with an otter asleep upon its back among the cushions on the sofa, forepaws in the air, and with the expression of tightly shut concentration that very small babies wear in sleep. On the stone slab beneath the chimney-piece are inscribed the words '*Non fatuum huc persecutus ignem*'—'It is no will-o'-the-wisp that I have followed here.' Beyond the door is the sea, whose waves break on the beach no more than a stone's throw distant, and encircling, mist-hung mountains. A little group of Greylag geese sweep past the window and alight upon the small carpet of green turf; but for the soft, contented murmur of their voices and the sounds of the sea and the waterfall there is utter silence. This place has been my home now for ten years and more, and wherever the changes of my life may lead me in the future it will remain my spiritual home until I die, a house to which one returns not with the certainty of welcoming fellow human beings, nor with the expectation of comfort and ease, but to a long familiarity in which every lichen-covered rock and rowan tree show known and reassuring faces.

I had not thought that I should ever come back to live in the West Highlands; when my earlier sojourn in the Hebrides had

3

come to an end it had in retrospect seemed episodic, and its finish uncompromisingly final. The thought of return had savoured of a jilted lover pleading with an indifferent mistress upon whom he had no further claim; it seemed to me then that it was indeed a will-o'-the-wisp that I had followed, for I had yet to learn that happiness can neither be achieved nor held by endeavour.

Looking back with distaste to the brashness of my late adolescence I perceive that I was an earnest member of the Celtic fringe, avid for tartan and twilight. This was no by-product of a Nationalistic outlook, nor could my yearnings have found outlet in that direction, for I was at that time also an arrant snob, and the movement seemed to me essentially plebeian; supported, moreover, by youths whose title to a foothold in the West Highlands was as controversial as my own. It was not to the company of such as these that I aspired; the healthier and more robust enthusiasm of tartaned hikers from the industrial cities inspired in me a nausea akin to that of Compton Mackenzie's Macdonald of Ben Nevis. It was not with the awe due to surviving dinosaurs that I viewed certain backwoods Highland chieftains with moustaches as long as their lineage, but with the enthusiastic reverence that the vintage-car cult accords to Bentleys of the 1920s. Nothing in my early life had led me to question the prescriptive rightness of the established order as it had been in the days of my grandparents; to me the West Highlands were composed of deer forests and hereditary chieftains, and the sheep, the hikers and the Forestry Commission were regrettable interlopers upon the romantic life of the indigenous aristocracy.

I was no whit abashed by the fact that I came of a lowland family who had been established in one spot for more than five hundred years, and that it was there and as a Galloway Scot that I had been born and brought up. It was a handicap, certainly, as was also my inability to perform Highland dances or to speak Gaelic; to learn would have been to acknowledge that I had not known before, and so would have been unthinkable. I did learn, however, to play a few tunes, very badly, on the bagpipes; I had had a Gaelic-speaking nurse; I had been brought up to wear a kilt—though of

4

shepherd's plaid; and, strongest card of all and probably what started the rot, my maternal grandmother had been a daughter of the Duke of Argyll, of MacCallum Mor himself. At Inveraray Castle and at Strachur on the opposite side of Loch Fyne I passed most of my long vacs from Oxford. Inveraray under the reign of the late Duke was a temple of twilight both Celtic and other, and its atmosphere was hardly calculated to cure my disease. The melancholy beauty of Strachur and Inveraray was for me still further complicated by the agonies of first love; I was well and truly pixillated, and I soaked myself in the works of Neil Munro and Maurice Walsh when I should have been laying the foundations of a literary education. All this was basically the outcome of an inherently romantic nature tinged with melancholy, for which a special home and uniform had clearly been prepared among the precipitous hills and sea lochs of the West Highlands.

There existed during my time at Oxford a curious clique of landed gentry so assertively un-urban that we affected a way of dressing quite unsuited to University life; at all times, for example, we wore tweed shooting suits and heavy shooting shoes studded with nails and dull with dubbin, and at our heels trotted spaniels or Labrador retrievers. Some of us were Englishmen, but the majority were Scots or those whose parents were in the habit of renting Highland shootings, and I have no doubt that the cult was akin to my own, for I remember that in the autumn term the rooms of its members were hung with the heads of stags killed during the vac. and there was endless talk of the Highlands. Most of us were, in fact, a species of privileged hiker, and we were also a striking example of the fact that aristocracy and education were no longer synonymous.

My own yearning for the Highlands was in those days as tormenting as an unconsummated love affair, for no matter how many stags I might kill or feudal castles inhabit I lacked an essential involvement; I was further from them than any immigrated Englishmen who planted one potato or raised one stone upon another. It is often those who dream of a *grande passion* who find it and suffer and are the sadder for it, and so it was with me, for when at last I came to the West Highlands by right of ownership and of effort they brought me to my knees and sent me away defeated and almost bankrupt. But during that five years' struggle the false image for which I had yearned had faded, and a truer one, less bedizened with tartan but no whit less beautiful, had taken its place.

Immediately after the war's end I bought the Island of Soay, some four thousand acres of relatively low-lying 'black' land cowering below the bare pinnacles and glacial corries of the Cuillin of Skye. There, seventeen miles by sea from the railway, I tried to found a new industry for the tiny and discontented population of the island, by catching and processing for oil the great basking sharks that appear in Hebridean waters during the summer months. I built a factory, bought boats and equipped them with harpoon guns, and became a harpoon gunner myself. For five years I worked in that landscape that before had been, for me, of a nebulous and cobwebby romance, and by the time it was all over and I was beaten I had in some way come to terms with the Highlands—or with myself, for perhaps in my own eyes I had earned the right to live among them, and the patent unauthenticity of the Maxwell tartan no longer disturbed me.

When the Soay venture was finished, the island and the boats sold, the factory demolished, and the population evacuated, I went to London and tried to earn my living as a portrait painter. One autumn I was staying with an Oxford contemporary who had bought an estate in the West Highlands, and in an idle moment after breakfast on a Sunday morning he said to me:

'Do you want a foothold on the west coast, now that you've lost Soay? If you're not too proud to live in a cottage, we've got an empty one, miles from anywhere. It's right on the sea and there's no road to it—Camusfeàrna, it's called. There's some islands, and an automatic lighthouse. There's been no one there for a long time, and I'd never get any of the estate people to live in it now. If you'll keep it up you're welcome to it.'

It was thus casually, ten years ago, that I was handed the keys of my home, and nowhere in all the West Highlands and islands have I seen any place of so intense or varied a beauty in so small a compass.

6

The road, single-tracked for the past forty miles, and reaching in the high passes a gradient of one in three, runs southwards a mile or so inland of Camusfeàrna and some four hundred feet above it. At the point on the road which is directly above the house there is a single cottage at the roadside, Druimfiaclach, the home of my friends and nearest neighbours, the MacKinnons. Inland from Druimfiaclach the hills rise steeply but in rolling masses to a dominating peak of more than three thousand feet, snow-covered or snow-dusted for the greater part of the year. On the other side, to the westward, the Isle of Skye towers across a three-mile-wide sound, and farther to the south the stark bastions of Rhum and the couchant lion of Eigg block the sea horizon. The descent to Camusfeàrna is so steep that neither the house nor its islands and lighthouse are visible from the road above, and that paradise within a paradise remains, to the casual road-user, unguessed. Beyond Druimfiaclach the road seems, as it were, to become dispirited, as though already conscious of its dead end at sea-level six miles farther on, caught between the terrifying massif of mountain scree overhanging it and the dark gulf of sea loch below.

Druimfiaclach is a tiny oasis in a wilderness of mountain and peat-bog, and it is a full four miles from the nearest roadside dwelling. An oasis, an eyrie; the windows of the house look west-ward over the Hebrides and over the tyrian sunsets that flare and fade behind their peaks, and when the sun has gone and the stars are bright the many lighthouses of the reefs and islands gleam and wink above the surf. In the westerly gales of winter the walls of Druimfiaclach rock and shudder, and heavy stones are roped to the corrugated iron roof to prevent it blowing away as other roofs here have gone before. The winds rage in from the Atlantic and the hail roars and batters on the windows and the iron roof, all hell let loose, but the house stands and the MacKinnons remain here, as, nearby, the forefathers of them both remained for many generations.

It seems strange to me now that there was a time when I did not know the MacKinnons, strange that the first time I came to live at Camusfeàrna I should have passed their house by a hundred yards and left my car by the roadside without greeting or acknowledgement of a dependence now long established. I remember seeing some small children staring from the house door; I cannot now recall my first meeting with their parents.

I left my car at a fank, a dry-stone enclosure for dipping sheep, close to the burn side, and because I was unfamiliar with the ill-defined footpath that is the more usual route from the road to Camusfeàrna, I began to follow the course of the burn downward. The burn has its source far back in the hills, near to the very summit of the dominant peak; it has worn a fissure in the scarcely sloping mountain wall, and for the first thousand feet of its course it part flows, part falls, chill as snow-water even in summer, between tumbled boulders and small multi-coloured lichens. Up there, where it seems the only moving thing besides the eagles, the deer and the ptarmigan, it is called the Blue Burn, but at the foot of the outcrop, where it passes through a reedy lochan and enters a wide glacial glen it takes the name of its destination—Allt na Feàrna, the Alder Burn. Here in the glen the clear topaz-coloured water rushes and twitters between low oaks, birches and alders, at whose feet the deep-cushioned green moss is stippled with bright toadstools of scarlet and purple and yellow, and in summer swarms of electric-blue dragonflies flicker and hover in the glades.

After some four miles the burn passes under the road at Druim-fiaclach, a stone's-throw from the fank where I had left my car. It was early spring when I came to live at Camusfeàrna for the first time, and the grass at the burn side was gay with thick-clustering primroses and violets, though the snow was still heavy on the high peaks and lay like lace over the lower hills of Skye across the Sound. The air was fresh and sharp, and from east to west and north to south there was not a single cloud upon the cold clear blue; against it, the still-bare birch branches were purple in the sun and the dark-banded stems were as white as the distant snows. On the sunny slopes grazing Highland cattle made a foreground to a landscape whose vivid colours had found no place on Landseer's palette. The rucksack bounced and jingled on my

8

shoulders; I was coming to my new home like one of the hikers whom long ago I had so much despised.

I was not quite alone, for in front of me trotted my dog Jonnie, a huge black-and-white springer spaniel whose father and grandfather before him had been my constant companions during an adolescence devoted largely to sport. We were brought up to shoot, and by the curious paradox that those who are fondest of animals become, in such an environment, most bloodthirsty at a certain stage of their development, shooting occupied much of my time and thoughts during my school and university years. Many people find an especial attachment for a dog whose companionship has bridged widely different phases in their lives, and so it was with Jonnie; he and his forebears had spanned my boyhood, maturity, and the war years, and though since then I had found little leisure nor much inclination for shooting, Jonnie adapted himself placidly to a new role, and I remember how during the shark fishery years he would, unprotesting, arrange himself to form a pillow for my head in the well of an open boat as it tossed and pitched in the waves.

Now Jonnie's plump white rump bounced and perked through the heather and bracken in front of me, as times without number at night I was in the future to follow its pale just-discernible beacon through the darkness from Druimfiaclach to Camusfeàrna.

Presently the burn became narrower, and afforded no foothold at its steep banks, then it tilted sharply seaward between rock walls, and below me I could hear the roar of a high waterfall. I climbed out from the ravine and found myself on a bluff of heather and red bracken, looking down upon the sea and upon Camusfeàrna.

The landscape and seascape that lay spread below me was of such beauty that I had no room for it all at once; my eye flickered from the house to the islands, from the white sands to the flat green pasture round the croft, from the wheeling gulls to the pale satin sea and on to the snow-topped Cuillins of Skye in the distance.

Immediately below me the steep hill-side of heather and ochre mountain grasses fell to a broad green field, almost an island, for

9

the burn flanked it at the right and then curved round seaward in a glittering horseshoe. The sea took up where the burn left off, and its foreshore formed the whole frontage of the field, running up nearest to me into a bay of rocks and sand. At the edge of this bay, a stone's throw from the sea on one side and the burn on the other, the house of Camusfeàrna stood unfenced in green grass among grazing black-faced sheep. The field, except immediately opposite to the house, sloped gently upwards from the sea, and was divided from it by a ridge of sand dunes grown over with pale marram grass and tussocky sea-bents. There were rabbits scampering on the short turf round the house, and out over the dunes the bullet heads of two seals were black in the tide.

Beyond the green field and the wide shingly outflow of the burn were the islands, the nearer ones no more than a couple of acres each, rough and rocky, with here and there a few stunted rowan trees and the sun red on patches of dead bracken. The islands formed a chain of perhaps half a mile in length, and ended in one as big as the rest put together, on whose seaward shore showed the turret of a lighthouse. Splashed among the chain of islands were small beaches of sand so white as to dazzle the eye. Beyond the islands was the shining enamelled sea, and beyond it again the rearing bulk of Skye, plum-coloured distances embroidered with threads and scrolls of snow.

Even at a distance Camusfeàrna house wore that strange look that comes to dwellings after long disuse. It is indefinable, and it is not produced by obvious signs of neglect; Camusfeàrna had few slates missing from the roof and the windows were all intact, but the house wore that secretive expression that is in some way akin to a young girl's face during her first pregnancy.

As I went on down the steep slope two other buildings came into view tucked close under the skirt of the hill, a byre facing Camusfeàrna across the green turf, and an older, windowless, croft at the very sea's edge, so close to the waves that I wondered how the house had survived. Later, I learned that the last occupants had been driven from it by a great storm which had brought the sea right into the house, so that they had been forced to make their escape by a window at the back.

At the foot of the hill the burn flowed calmly between an avenue of single alders, though the sound of unseen waterfalls was loud in the rock ravine behind me. I crossed a solid wooden bridge with stone piers, and a moment later I turned the key in Camus-feàrna door for the first time.

2

THERE WAS not one stick of furniture in the house; there was no water and no lighting, and the air inside struck chill as a mortuary, but to me it was Xanadu. There was much more space in the house than I had expected. There were two rooms on the ground floor, a parlour and a living-kitchen, besides a little 'back kitchen' or scullery, and two rooms and a landing upstairs. The house was entirely lined with varnished pitch pine, in the manner of the turn of the century.

I had brought with me on my back the essentials of living for a day or two while I prospected—a bedding roll, a Primus stove with a little fuel, candles, and some tinned food. I knew that something to sit upon would present no problems, for my five years' shark hunting round these coasts had taught me that every west-facing beach is littered with fish-boxes. Stacks of fish-boxes arranged to form seats and tables were the mainstay of Camus-feàrna in those early days, and even now, despite the present comfort of the house, they form the basis of much of its furniture, though artifice and padding have done much to disguise their origin.

Ten years of going into retreat at Camusfeàrna have taught me, too, that if one waits long enough practically every imaginable household object will sooner or later turn up on the beaches within a mile of the house, and beachcombing retains for me now the same fascination and eager expectancy that it held then. After a westerly or south-westerly gale one may find almost anything. Fish-boxes—mostly stamped with the names of Mallaig, Buckie, or Lossiemouth firms, but sometimes from France or Scandinavia —are too common to count, though they are still gathered, more from habit than from need. Fish baskets, big open two-handled baskets of withy, make firewood baskets and waste-paper baskets. Intact wooden tubs are a rarity, and I have found only three in my years here; it has amused me wryly to see cocktail bars in England whose proprietors have through whimsy put them to use as stools as I have by necessity.

A Robinson Crusoe or Swiss Family Robinson instinct is latent in most of us, perhaps from our childhood games of house-building, and since I came to Camusfeàrna ten years ago I find myself scanning every weird piece of flotsam or jetsam and con-sidering what useful purpose it might be made to serve. As a beachcomber of long standing now I have been amazed to find that one of the commonest of all things among jetsam is the rubber hot-water bottle. They compete successfully—in the long straggling line of brown sea-wrack dizzy with jumping sand-hoppers—with odd shoes and empty boot polish and talcum powder tins, with the round corks that buoy lobster-pots and nets, even with the ubiquitous skulls of sheep and deer. A surprising number of the hot-water bottles are undamaged, and Camus-feàrna is by now overstocked with them, but from the damaged ones one may cut useful and highly functional table mats.

At the beginning, however, there was no table to protect, and after my first days at Camusfeàrna it seemed clear that I should have to import at least one small load of essential furniture. This was not an easy matter, for there was no road approach, and I was some fifteen miles by sea from the nearest village to which I could have furniture sent. (Because of the long sea lochs that, like Norwegian fiords, cut deep into the west coast, that same village is one hundred and twenty miles by road.) At length I motored to Lochailort Inn—a hundred miles—whose highly individual proprietor, Uilleamena Macrae, I had come to know well during my shark-fishing years. Uilleamena was a very beautiful Lewis woman of humble origin, but she had been to Hollywood as an actress in the early days of silent films; she had been a medium for Conan Doyle's spiritualistic experiments; she had been taught logic—rather unsuccessfully—by an uncle who had become a professor in America; she had friends, real ones, in many high places. During the war, when she was already in late middle age, she married, very briefly, the contractor who was repairing the road outside her door; in a few months he was called up and killed, and Uilleamena reverted to her maiden name and never again mentioned her *mésalliance*. She was, I think, one of the warmest, most human, most delightful, and, perhaps, most domineering people I have ever known, and her faults were all on the surface. As an innkeeper she was unorthodox and capricious; lunch might cost anything between two shillings and a pound, according to her mood (or sometimes there would be no lunch at all, if she did not feel like cooking or did not care for the look of the visitors); the bar would remain closed for days or even weeks because she had forgotten to order new stock, and the same applied to the petrol pump; she was more concerned with the welfare of a host of animals ranging from a parrot (I can still hear those two screeching 'hullo' to each other in demoniac crescendo) to geese and Shetland ponies than with that of stranger tourists (she told me that she had once given chicken-food to some American visitors, telling them it was porridge, and that they had asked for more); yet with all that, her personality was so spontaneous and vital and endearing that her death a few years ago made a hole in more hearts than she would have known. She left a truly phenomenal amount of debts behind her, but it was perhaps a measure of her personality that she was able to owe her grocer £3,000.

Uilleamena sold me some really frightful furniture for Camusfeàrna—two small chests whose drawers open and close only under the most careful coaxing, two kitchen tables, a bed, three hard kitchen chairs, and a thread-bare Brussels carpet. I prefer not to think what these outrages had finally cost me by the time they had travelled by rail and then fifteen miles in a hired launch by sea. They were the last bulk of furniture that ever came into Camusfeàrna; the rest has just grown, found on the beach or constructed by ingenious friends who have stayed here, and importations have been confined to what can be carried down the hill. Into this category fall a surprising number of objects that may be used to convert fish-boxes into apparent furniture. Half of one of the kitchen walls, for example, is now occupied by a very large sofa; that is to say it appears to be a sofa, but in fact it is all fish-boxes, covered with sheet foam rubber under a corduroy cover and many cushions. Next to it is a tall rectangle, draped over with a piece of material that was once the seat-cover of my cabin in the *Sea Leopard*, my chief shark-hunting boat; lift aside this relic and you are looking into a range of shelves filled with shoes—the whole structure is made of five fish-boxes with their sides knocked out. The same system, this time of orange-boxes from the shore and fronted by some very tasteful material from Primavera, holds shirts and sweaters in my bedroom, and looks entirely respectable. The art of fish-box furniture should be more widely cultivated; in common with certain widely advertised makes of contemporary furniture it has the peculiar advantage that one may add unit to unit indefinitely.

There came a time, in my second or third year at the house, when I said, 'There's only one thing we really lack now—a clothes-basket,' and a few weeks later a clothes-basket came up on the beach, a large stately clothes-basket, completely un-damaged.

Whether it is because the furnishings of these rooms have grown around me year by year since that first afternoon when I entered the chill and empty house, each room as bare as a weathered bone, or because of my deep love for Camusfeàrna and all that sur-rounds it, it is to me now the most relaxing house that I know, and guests, too, feel it a place in which they are instantly at ease. Even in this small matter of furniture there is also a continuous sense of anticipation; it is as though a collector of period furniture might on any morning find some rare and important piece lying waiting to be picked up on the street before his door.

There is much pathos in the small jetsam that lies among the sea-wrack and drifted timber of the long tide-lines; the fire-blackened transom of a small boat; the broken and wave-battered children's toys; a hand-carved wooden egg-cup with the name 'John' carefully incised upon it; the scattered skeleton of a small dog, the collar with an illegible nameplate lying among the whitened bones, long since picked clean by the ravens and the hooded crows. To me the most personal poignancy was in my search one morning that first year for a suitable piece of wood from which to fashion a bread-board. A barrel top would be ideal, I thought, if I could find one intact, and very soon I did, but when I had it in my hands I turned it over to read the letters I.S.S.F., Island of Soay Shark Fisheries—the only thing the sea has ever given me back for all that I poured into it during those five years of Soay.

Some pieces of jetsam are wholly enigmatic, encouraging the most extravagant exercise of fantasy to account for their existence. A ten-foot-long bamboo pole, to which have been affixed by a combination of careful, seaman-like knots and the lavish use of insulating tape three blue pennants bearing the words 'Shell' and 'B.P.'; this has exercised my imagination since first I found it. A prayer flag made by a Lascar seaman?—a distress signal, pitifully inadequate, constructed over many hours adrift in an open boat surrounded by cruising sharks or tossed high on the crests of Atlantic rollers a thousand miles from land? I have found no satisfactory solution. Two broom-handles, firmly tied into the form of a cross by the belt from a woman's plastic macintosh; a scrap of sailcloth with the words 'not yet' scrawled across it in blue paint; a felt Homburg hat so small that it appeared to have been made for a diminutive monkey—round these and many others one may weave idle tapestries of mystery.

But it is not only on such man-made objects as these that the imagination builds to evoke drama, pathos, or remembered splendour. When one is much alone one's vision becomes more extensive; from the tide-wrack rubbish-heap of small bones and dry, crumpled wings, relics of lesser lives, rise images the brighter for being unconfined by the physical eye. From some feathered mummy, stained and thin, soars the spinning lapwing in the white March morning; in the surface crust of rotting weed, where the foot explodes a whirring puff of flies, the withered fins and scales hold still, intrinsically, the sway and dart of glittering shoals among the tide-swung sea-tangle; smothered by the mad parabolic energy of leaping sand-hoppers the broken antlers of a stag re-form and move again high in the bare, stony corries and the October moonlight.

Comparatively little that is thrown up by the waves comes ashore at Camusfeàrna itself, for the house stands on a south-facing bay in a west-facing coast line, and it gains, too, a little shelter from the string of islands that lead out from it to the lighthouse. To the north and south the coast is rock for the most part, but opening here and there to long gravel beaches which the prevailing westerly gales pile high with the sea's litter. It is a fierce shoreline, perilous with reef and rock, and Camusfeàrna with its snow-white sand beaches, green close-cropped turf, and low white lighthouse has a welcoming quality enhanced by the dark, rugged coastline on either side.

It is a coast of cliffs and of caves, deep commodious caves that have their entrances, for the most part, well above the tides' level, for over the centuries the sea has receded, and between the cliffs the shingle of its old beaches lies bare. Until recently many of these caves were regularly inhabited by travelling pedlars, of whom there were many, for shops were far distant and communications virtually non-existent. They were welcome among the local people, these pedlars, for besides what they could sell they brought news from far-away villages and of other districts in which they travelled; they fulfilled the function of provincial newspapers, and the inhabitants of wild and lonely places awaited their coming with keen anticipation.

One of these men made his home and headquarters in a cave close to Camusfeàrna, a man who had been, of all improbable professions, a jockey. Andrew Tait was his real name, but as a deserter from the army he had changed it to Joe Wilson, and Joe's Cave his erstwhile home remains, even on the maps, though it is many years past since an angry people lit fires to crack the rock roof and banish him from that shore.

Joe was popular at first, for he was a likeable enough man, and if he and his cave consort Jeannie had never heard the wedding service a cave was perhaps safer than a glass-house if there were any stones to be thrown. Such pebbles that came his way seem mainly to have been on the question of his desertion. Jeannie was no slut nor Joe a slum-maker, and their troglodyte life was a neat and orderly affair, with a clean white tablecloth laid over the fish-box table for meals, meals that were of fish and crustaceans and every manner of edible shell. They walled in the front of their cave and built steps from it down to the sea, and even now the little runway where they drew up their boat is still free from boulders.

Only one thing marred their littoral idyll; both Jeannie and Joe were over-fond of the bottle. Jeannie held the purse-strings, and despite her own indulgence she was the wiser of the two. She would spend so much on drink and no more, but every time the two drank they quarrelled, and when Joe got past a certain point he would fight her for the money.

One night they had, as was their custom, rowed the four miles to the village pub, and there they began to drink in company with another pedlar, a simpleton, named John MacQueen, whom people called The Pelican. The Pelican was a player of the fiddle, and together they stayed late at the inn, bickering and drinking to the music of his strings.

What followed no one knows truly to this day, but it was the end of their Eden, the end of Jeannie and of Joe's Cave. Joe returned to the village in the morning proclaiming over and over again that Jeannie was 'Killt and droont, killt and droont.' Their boat was washed up ten miles to the south, half full of water, and in it was the dead body of Jeannie; the pocket of her skirt had been torn off, and there was no money about her. Police came from the nearest township, but though local feeling ran high against Joe and The Pelican the details of Jeannie's death remained unsolved, and no charge of murder was brought against them. It seemed clear that Jeannie had been knocked out before she drowned; some, those who stood by Joe, said that she had fallen into the sea after a blow and then drowned; others that Joe and The Pelican had beaten her senseless in a drunken rage, had half-filled the boat with water, and then set Jeannie adrift to drown.

Whatever the truth, the people of the neighbourhood—if such it could be called, for Joe had no neighbours—believed that they had a monster in their midst; they came and built great fires in his cave, and set ablaze the heather of the hillside above it, so that the heat split the rock and the outer part of the cave fell, and Joe was left a homeless wanderer. He died years ago, but on the floor beneath the fire-blackened rock still lie small relics of his life with Jeannie, mouldering shoes, scraps of metal, a filligree tracery of rusted iron that was once a kettle. Above, on the ledges that formed the cornice of his dwelling, the rock-doves have made their homes, and their feathers float down upon the ruined hearth.

Pedlars of the traditional type were rare by the time I began to live at Camusfeàrna; their place had been taken by Indians, often importunate, who from time to time toured the roadside dwellings with small vans full of cheap materials. The local inhabitants, unused to high-pressure doorstep salesmanship, mistook these methods for affrontery; not all of the vendors were of savoury nature, but even the most innocuous were regarded with a wary suspicion. I met only one of Joe's lost tribe, and he has died since, hastened to the churchyard by a life-long predilection for drinking methylated spirits. He was, I think, in his early sixties when I first encountered him; he told me then that the perils of his preferred liquor were greatly exaggerated, for he had been indulging for forty years and only now was his eyesight beginning to suffer. He confided, however, that it was an inconvenient craving, for most ironmongers throughout the length and breadth of the West Highlands had been warned against supplying him, and he had been driven to the most elaborate of subterfuges to keep his cellar stocked. It was, perhaps, as well for him that he died before electricity came to the remote and outlying areas, for then, as I discovered to my cost, methylated spirits became virtually un-obtainable.

The cave-dwelling pedlars had not always been the only inhabitants of the Camusfeàrna coastline, for before the Clearances in the early nineteenth century—whose cruelty and injustice are still a living ancestral memory in a great part of the West High-lands and Hebrides—there had been a thriving community of some two hundred people not far from where Camusfeàrna house now stands. The descendants of one of these families still live in California, where their forebears settled when driven from their homes, and of them is told one of the few local tales of 'second sight' that I have come across in the district.

The children of the old settlement at Camusfeàrna used to walk the five miles to the village school every morning and five miles home again at night; each child, too, had in winter to provide his contribution to the school fire, and they would set off before dawn for the long trudge with a creel of peats on their backs. One night this family had given shelter to an old pedlar, and as he watched the two sons of the house making ready their load in the morning he turned to their parents and said, 'Many a green sea they will go over, but many a green sea will go over them.' The boys came of a sea-faring line, and when they grew up they too followed the sea; one became a captain and the other a first mate, but both were drowned.

The tumbled, briar-grown ruins of the old village are scattered round the bay and down the shore, but the people are gone and the pedlars are gone and the house at Camusfeàrna stands alone.

Whereas the stories of 'second sight' are comparatively few, and refer most commonly to past generations, it should be realized that this bears no relation at all either to current credence in the faculty or to the number of people who are still believed to possess it. Quite contrary to general opinion, a person having or believing him or herself to have this occult power is extremely reticent about it, usually afraid of it, and conceals it from all but his most intimate friends. This is not because he is afraid of mockery or disbelief in the sense that his neighbour will say 'Behold this dreamer', but because men fear proof of a power beyond their own, and are uncomfortable in the company of one who claims or admits to it. These people who are convinced of being endowed with what is now more usually called extra-sensory perception are also frightened of what their own clair-voyance may show them, and it seems that they would willingly exchange their lot for that of the common man. Only when they are convinced that their gift can at that moment be turned to benign use are they prepared to call it voluntarily into play. My impression is that a deep, fundamental belief in the existence of 'second sight' is practically universal throughout the Western Highlands and the Hebrides, even among intelligent and well-read people, and that the few scoffers are paying lip-service to a sceptical sophistication they do not share. Circumstantial tales of other less controversial matters survive in the oral tradition with but little change in these districts to which literacy came late in history, and there is no reason to assume that those concerning 'second sight' should have suffered disproportionate distortion.

My nearest neighbour at Camusfeàrna, Calum Murdo Mac-Kinnon, of whom I shall have more to say presently, comes of Skye stock, and tells a tale of his forebears which by its very simplicity is hard to ascribe to past invention. In the days of his great-grandfather a boy was drowned at sea, fishing in the bay before the village, and his mother became distraught with the desire to recover her son's body and give it Christian burial. Some half-dozen boats with grappling irons cruised to and fro all day over the spot where he had been lost, but found nothing. The talk of all the village was naturally centred on the subject, and in the late evening Calum Murdo's great-grandfather, over eighty years of age, infirm and totally blind, learned for the first time of all that had taken place. At length he said, 'If they will take me to the knoll overlooking the bay in the morning I will tell them where the body lies. They will need just the one boat.' The searchers obeyed him, and in the morning he was carried to the summit of the knoll by his grandson, who brought with him a plaid with which to signal at command. For more than half an hour the boat rowed to and fro in the bay below them with grapples hanging ready, but the old man sat with his blind head in his hands and said never a word. Suddenly he cried in a strong voice, '*Togh an tonnag!*—Hoist the plaid!' His grandson did so, and the grapples sank and returned to the surface with the body of the drowned boy.

It is easier to be sceptical when one is not in the Hebrides; easier when one's vision is not clarified—or obscured—by the common sense of one's fellow men.

Very little survives in legend from the early inhabitants of Camusfeàrna; surprisingly little when one comes to consider that in all likelihood the community existed for thousands of years. The earliest stories date, probably, from the Middle Ages, and one of these tells of a wild sea reiver, born in the bay, who harried the coast to the southward—notably the Island of Mull, with its many secret harbours and well-hid anchorages—in a galleon, one of whose sides was painted black and the other white; an attempt, presumably, to refute description or to undermine morale by reports that in aggregate might give the impression of a pirate fleet. Whatever his tactics, they seem to have been successful, for he is said to have returned to Camusfeàrna and to have died, in old age, a natural death.

In the British Isles it is a strange sensation to lie down to sleep knowing that there is no human being within a mile and a half in any direction, that apart from one family there is none for three times that distance. Indeed few people ever have the experience, for the earth's surface is so overrun with mankind that where land is habitable it is inhabited; and whereas it is not difficult to pitch a camp in those circumstances it is very rare to be between four permanent walls that one may call one's home. It brings a sense of isolation that is the very opposite of the loneliness a stranger finds in a city, for that loneliness is due to the proximity of other humans and the barriers between him and them, to the knowledge of being alone among them, with every inch of the walls wounding and every incommunicable stranger planting a separate bandillo. But to be quite alone where there are no other human beings is sharply exhilarating; it is as though some pressure had suddenly been lifted, allowing an intense awareness of one's surroundings, a sharpening of the senses, and an intimate recognition of the teeming sub-human life around one. I experienced it first as a very young man, travelling alone, on the tundra three hundred miles north of the Arctic Circle, and there was the added strangeness of nights as light as noon, so that only the personal fact of sleep divided night from day; paradoxically, for the external circumstances were the very opposite, I had the same or an allied sensation during the heavy air-raids in 1940, as though life were suddenly stripped of inessentials such as worries about money and small egotistical ambitions and one was left facing an ultimate essential.

That first night as I lay down to sleep in the bare kitchen of Camusfeàrna I was aware of the soft thump of rabbits' feet about the sand dune warren at the back of the house, the thin squeak of hawking bats, woken early by the warm weather from their winter hibernation, and the restless piping of oyster-catchers waiting for the turn of the tide; these were middle-distance sounds against the muffled roar of the waterfall that in still weather is the undertone to all other sound at Camusfeàrna.

I slept that night with my head pillowed upon Jonnie's soft fleece-like flank, as years before I had been wont to in open boats.

The first thing that I saw in the morning, as I went down to the burn for water, was a group of five stags, alert but unconcerned, staring from the primrose bank just beyond the croft wall. Two of them had cast both horns, for it was the end of the first week in April, two had cast one, but the fifth stag still carried both, wide, long and strong, with seven points one side and six on the other, a far nobler head than ever I had seen during my years of bloodthirstiness. I came to know these stags year by year, for they were a part of a group that passed every winter low in the

23

Camusfeàrna burn, and Morag MacKinnon used to feed them at Druimfiaclach—a little surreptitiously, for they were outside the forest fence and on the sheep ground. Monarch, she called the thirteen-pointer, and though he never seemed to break out to the rut in autumn I think he must have sired at least one stag-calf, for

in the dark last year the headlights of my car lit up a partially stunned stag that had leapt at the concrete posts of the new forestry plantation fence, trying to get down to Camusfeàrna, and the head, though no more than a royal, was the very double of Monarch's wide sweep. I came near to killing him, for I thought that he was a stag wounded and lost by a stalking party from the lodge that day, but dazed as he was he managed to stagger out of the headlights' beam before I could get the rifle from its case.

I miss the stags that used to winter close to the house, for now there are young trees planted over the hill face between Camusfeàrna and Druimfiaclach, and the deer have been forced back behind the forest fence, so that there is none, save an occasional interloper, within a mile of the bay. In the first winter that I was at Camusfeàrna I would wake to see from the window a frieze of their antlers etching the near skyline, and they were in some way important to me, as were the big footprints of the wildcats in the soft sand at the burn's edge, the harsh cry of the ravens, and the round shiny seals' heads in the bay below the house. These creatures were my neighbours.

English visitors who have come to Camusfeàrna are usually

struck inarticulate by the desolate grandeur of the landscape and
the splendour of pale blue and gold spring mornings, but they are
entirely articulate in their amazement at the variety of wild life
by which I am surrounded. Many Englishmen are, for example,
quite unaware that wildcats are common animals in the West
Highlands, and assume, when one refers to them, that one is
speaking of domestic cats run wild, not of the tawny lynx-like
ferals that had their den, that and every other year, within two
hundred yards of my door. They bear as much relation to the
domestic cat as does a wolf to a terrier; they were here before our
first uncouth ancestors came to live in the caves below the cliffs,
and they are reputedly untameable. When I first came here the
estate on whose land the house stood had long waged war upon
the wildcats, and a tree by the deer-larder of the lodge, four miles
away, was decorated with their banded tails hanging like monstrous willow catkins from its boughs. Now, since the estate has
turned from general agriculture to forestry, the wildcats are
protected, for they are the worst enemy of the voles, who are in
turn the greatest destroyers of the newly planted trees. Under this
benign régime the number of wildcats has marvellously increased.
The males sometimes mate with domestic females, but the offspring rarely survives, either because the sire returns to kill the
kittens as soon as they are born, and so expunge the evidence of
his peasant wenching, or because of the distrust in which so many
humans hold the taint of the untameable. It is the wild strain that
is dominant, in the lynx-like appearance, the extra claw, and the
feral instinct; and the few half-breeds that escape destruction
usually take to the hills and the den life of their male ancestors. An
old river-watcher at Lochailort, who for some reason that now
eludes me was known as Tipperary, told me that one night,
awoken by the caterwauling outside, he had gone to the door
with a torch and in its beam had seen his own black-and-white
she-cat in the fierce embrace of a huge wild tom. Thereafter he
had waited eagerly for the birth of the kittens. When the time
came she made her nest in the byre, and all that day he waited for
the first birth, but at nightfall she had not yet brought forth. In
the small hours of the morning he became conscious of piteous

mewing at his door, and opened it to find his cat carrying in her mouth one wounded and dying kitten. In the dark background he heard a savage sound of worrying and snarling, and flashing his torch towards the byre he saw the wild tom in the act of killing a kitten. There was a green ember-glow of eyes, the flash of a big bottle-brush tail, and then the torch lit up nothing more but a pathetic trail of mangled new-born kittens. The single survivor, whom the mother had tried to carry to the house for sanctuary, died a few minutes later.

Wildcats grow to an enormous size, at least double that of the very largest domestic cat; this year there is one who leaves close to the house Homeric droppings of dimensions that would make an Alsatian wolfhound appear almost constipated. It is comparatively rarely that one sees the animals themselves in the daytime, for they are creatures of the dark and the starlight. Once I caught one accidentally in a rabbit snare, a vast tom with ten rings to his tail, and that first year at Camusfeàrna I twice saw the kittens at play in the dawn, frolicking among the primroses and budding birch on the bank beyond the croft wall. They looked beautiful, very soft and fluffy, and almost gentle; there was no hint of the ferocity that takes a heavy annual toll of lambs and red-deer calves. Before man exterminated the rabbits they were the staple food both of the big leggy hill foxes and of these low-ground wildcats, and every morning I would see the heavily indented pad-marks in the sand at the burrow mouths. But now the rabbits have gone and the lambs are still here in their season, and where there has been a strong lamb at dusk, at dawn there are raw bones and a fleece like a bloodstained swab in a surgery. Then come the ravens from the sea cliffs, and the hooded crows, the ubiquitous grey-mantled scavengers, and by nightfall there is nothing to show for those slow months in the womb but white skeleton and a scrap of soft, soiled fleece that seems no bigger than a handkerchief.

Among the mammals it is, next to the wildcats, the seals that surprise my southern visitors most. Right through the summer months they are rarely out of sight, and, being unmolested at Camusfeàrna, they become very tame. In the evenings they will follow a dinghy through the smooth sunset-coloured water, their heads emerging ever nearer and nearer until they are no more than a boat's length away. It is only a change in rhythm that frightens them; one must row steadily onwards as if intent on one's own business and unconcerned with theirs. The brown seals, with their big round skulls and short, dog-like noses, are everywhere, and I have counted more than a hundred in an hour's run down the shore in the dinghy; besides these, which breed locally, the Atlantic seals stay round the islands from May till early autumn, when they return to their scattered and comparatively few breeding rocks. The Atlantic seals that spend the summer at Camusfeàrna probably breed on the rocks west of Canna, by a long way the nearest to me of their colonies. They are never in large parties away from the breeding grounds; through the long still days of summer when the sea is smooth as silk and the sun is hot on the lichened rocks above the tide they loaf about the Camusfeàrna islands in twos and threes, usually bulls, eating largely of the rock fish and storing up energy to be used recklessly on their harems in the autumn, for during the rut the bulls may not feed for many weeks. To one who sees them for the first time the Atlantic seals seem vast; a big bull is some nine feet long and weighs nearly half a ton. They are splendid beasts, but to me they lack the charm of the little brown seal with its less dignified habits, inquisitive and dog-like. Once, on the rocks off Rhu Arisaig, I picked up a brown seal pup no more than a day or so old—he had the soft white baby coat that is more often shed in the womb, and he seemed for all the world like a toy designed to please a child. He was warm and tubby and not only unafraid but squirmingly affectionate, and I set him down again with some reluctance. But he was not to be so easily left, for as I moved off he came shuffling and humping along at my heels. After a few minutes of trying to shake him off I tried dodging and hiding behind rocks, but he discovered me with amazing agility. Finally I scrambled down to the boat and rowed quickly away, but after twenty yards he was there beside me muzzling an oar. I was in desperation to know what to do with this unexpected foundling whose frantic mother was now snorting twenty yards away, when suddenly he responded to one of her calls and the two went off together, the pup no doubt to receive the lecture of his life.

The red-deer calves, too, have no natural fear of man during their first days of life, and if in June one stumbles upon a calf lying dappled and sleek among the long green bracken stems one must avoid handling him if one wants to make a clean get-away. I used to pet them and fondle them before I knew better, and my efforts to leave led to more frenzied games of hide-and-seek than with the seal pup, while a distracted hind stamped and barked un-availingly. But while the calves during those first uninstructed days display no instinctive fear of humans, they are from the first terrified of their natural enemies, the eagles, the wildcats and the foxes. I have seen a hind trying to defend her calf from an eagle, rearing up with her ears back and slashing wickedly with her fore-hooves each time he stooped with an audible rush of wind through his great upswept pinions; if one hoof had struck home she would have brought him down disembowelled, but though she never touched more than a wingtip the eagle grew wary and finally sailed off down the glen, the sun gleaming whitely on the burnish of his mantle.

It is the helpless red-deer calves that are the staple food of the hill foxes in June, and the young lambs in April and May, but what they live on for the rest of the year now that the rabbits have gone and the blue mountain hares become so scarce, remains a mystery to me. Possibly they eat more seldom than we imagine, and certainly mice form a large part of their diet. Some years ago I went out with a stalker to kill hill foxes after lambing time. The foxes' cairn was some two thousand feet up the hill, and we left at dawn, before the sun was up over hills that were still all snow at their summits, silhouetted against a sky that was apple-green with tenuous scarlet streamers. The cairn, a big tumble of granite boulders in a fissure of the hill-side, was just below the snowline, and by the time we reached it the sun had lifted in a golden glare over the high tops. The terriers went into the cairn and we shot the vixen as she bolted, and the dogs killed and brought out the five cubs; but of the dog fox there was no sign at all. We found his footprints in a peat hag a few hundred yards below, going downhill, and he had not been galloping but quietly trotting, so we concluded that he had left the cairn some time before we had reached it and was probably unaware of anything amiss. We sat down under cover to wait for his return.

We waited all day. The spring breeze blew fresh in our faces from where the sea and the islands lay spread out far below us, and we could see the ring-net boats putting out for the first of the summer herring. All day there was very little movement on the hill; once a party of stags in early velvet crossed the lip of the corrie on our right, and once an eagle sailed by within a stone's throw, to bank sharply and veer off with a harsh rasp of air between the quills as his searching eye found us. In the evening it became chilly, and when the sun was dipping over the Outer Hebrides and the snow-shadows had turned to a deep blue, we began to think of moving. We were starting to gather up our things when my eye caught a movement in the peat hags below us. The dog fox was trotting up hill to the cairn, quite unsuspicious, and carrying something in his jaws. The rifle killed him stone dead at fifty yards, and we went down to see what he had been carrying; it was a nest of pink new-born mice—all he had found to bring home in a long day's hunting for his vixen and five cubs.

At first sight it is one of the enigmas of the country around Camusfeàrna, this great number of predators surviving with so little to prey upon; in the air the eagles, buzzards, falcons, ravens and hooded crows, and on the ground the wildcats, foxes, badgers and pine martens. There is no doubt that a surprising number of the animal species spend much time during the off seasons—when there are no young creatures to feed on—in my own hobby of beachcombing. In the soft sand around the tide-wrack I come constantly upon the footprints of wildcats, badgers and foxes. Sometimes they find oiled seabirds, sometimes the carcase of a sheep, fallen from one of the green cliff ledges that throughout the West Highlands form such well-baited and often fatal traps, or of a stag that has tottered down from the March snowdrifts to seek seaweed as the only uncovered food, or they may creep up upon sleeping oyster-catchers and curlews as they wait in the dark for the turn of the tide. But whatever they find it is to the shore that the fanged creatures come at night, and at times, perhaps, they find little, for I have seen undigested sand-hoppers in the droppings of both wildcats and foxes.

The ravens and hooded crows, though they will peck out the eyes of a living lamb or deer calf if he is weak, are in fact offal feeders for the greater part of the time. The hoodies spend much of their time about the shore in the late summer and midwinter, opening mussels by carrying them up to house-height and dropping them to smash on the rocks, but at most other seasons of

the year there are routine harvests for them to gather elsewhere. In the back-end of winter, when the ground is as yet unstirred by spring, the old stags that have wintered poorly grow feeble and die in the snowdrifts and the grey scavengers squawk and squabble over the carcases; a little later, when the first warmth comes, and the hinds interrupt their grazing to turn their heads and nibble irritably at their spines, the hoodies strut and pick around them, gobbling the fat warble-grubs that emerge from under the deer-hides and fall to the ground. When the lambing season comes they quarter the ground for the afterbirths, and from then on there are the eggs and young of every bird lesser than themselves.

Of my human neighbours, the MacKinnons, I have so far said little. Calum Murdo MacKinnon is always given both his Christian names, for there are so many Calum MacKinnons in the district that Calum alone would be ambiguous; there are so many Murdos as to make that name by itself ineffective too; and there are so many Murdo Calums, which is the true sequence of his names, that to retain his identity he has had to invert them. This was a common practice under the clan system, and is still the general rule in many parts of the West Highlands, where the clan names still inhabit their old territory. Sometimes he was abbreviated to 'Calum the Road' (in the same way I have known elsewhere a 'John the Hearse', a 'Duncan the Lorry', a 'Ronald the Shooter' and a 'Ronald Donald the Dummy'—the last not in any aspersion upon his human reality but because he was dumb). But the necessity for this strict taxonomy is a strange situation for one whose nearest neighbour other than myself is four miles distant.

Calum Murdo, then, is a small wiry man in middle age, who, when I first came to Camusfeàrna, had for long been the road-mender responsible for several miles of the single-track road on either side of Druimfiaclach. It might be expected that a Highlander living in this remarkable isolation would have few topics of conversation beyond the small routine of his own existence; one would not, for example, expect him to be able to quote the greater part of the *Golden Treasury*, to have read most of the classics, to have voluble and well-informed views on politics national and international, or to be a subscriber to the *New Statesman*. Yet these were the facts, and I fear it must have been a sad disappointment to Calum Murdo to find his new neighbour, of a supposedly higher educational level, to be on many subjects less well informed than himself. He would impart to me much fascinating and anecdotal information on a host of subjects, and would close every session with a rounded formula: 'And now, Major, an educated man like yourself will be fair sick of listening to the haverings of an old prole.' Over a period of ten years he has contributed much to my education.

With Calum Murdo's wife Morag, a woman of fine-drawn iron beauty softened by humour, I found an immediate common ground in a love of living creatures. One reads and hears much at second hand of the spiritual descendants of St. Francis and of St. Cuthbert, those who experience an immediate intimate communication with bird and beast, and of whom wild things feel no fear, but I had never encountered one of them in the flesh until I met Morag, and I had become a little sceptical of their existence.

What little success I myself have with animals is due, I think, solely to patience, experience, and a conscious effort to put myself in the animal's position, but I do not think that any of these things have been necessary to Morag. She frankly finds more to like and to love in animals than in human beings, and they respond to her immediately as if she were one of themselves, with a trust and respect that few of us receive from our own kind. I am convinced that there exists between her and them some *rapport* that is not for the achievement, even by long perseverance, of the bulk of those humans who would wish it. It would not, perhaps, be difficult to find more understandable explanations for individual cases in which, with her, this *rapport* seems apparent, but it is the number of these cases, and the consistency with which the animals' behaviour departs from its established pattern towards mankind, that convinces me of something not yet explainable in existing terms.

A single instance will be enough for illustration. Across the road from the MacKinnons' door is a reedy hill-side lochan some hundred yards long by fifty wide, and every winter the wild swans, the whoopers, would come to it as they were driven south by Arctic weather, to stay often for days and sometimes for weeks. Morag loved the swans, and from the green door of her house she would call a greeting to them several times a day, so that they came to know her voice, and never edged away from her to the other side of the lochan as they did when other human figures appeared on the road. One night she heard them restless and calling, the clear bugle voices muffled and buffeted by the wind, and when she opened the door in the morning she saw that there was something very much amiss. The two parent birds were at the near edge of the loch, fussing, if anything so graceful and dignified as a wild swan can be said to fuss, round a cygnet that seemed in some way to be captive at the margin of the reeds. Morag began to walk towards the loch, calling to them all the while as she was wont. The cygnet flapped and struggled and beat the water piteously with his wings, but he was held fast below the peaty surface, and all the while the parents, instead of retreating before Morag, remained calling at his side. Morag waded out, but the loch bottom is soft and black, and she was sinking thigh deep before she realized that she could not reach the cygnet. Then suddenly he turned and struggled towards her, stopped the thrashing of his wings, and was still. Groping in the water beneath him, Morag's hand came upon a wire, on which she pulled until she was able to feel a rusty steel trap clamped to the cygnet's leg, a trap set for a fox, and fastened to a long wire so that he might drown himself and die the more quickly. Morag lifted the cygnet from the water; he lay passive in her arms while she eased the jaws open, and as she did this the two parents swam right in and remained one on either side of her, as tame, as she put it, as domestic ducks; neither did they swim away when she put the cygnet undamaged on to the water and began to retrace her steps.

The swans stayed for a week or more after that, and now they would not wait for her to call to them before greeting her; every time she opened her door their silver-sweet, bell-like voices chimed to her from the lochan across the road. If Yeats had possessed the same strange powers as Morag, his nine and fifty swans would perhaps not have suddenly mounted, and his poem would not have been written.

It was not through childlessness that Morag had turned to animals, as do so many spinsters, for she had three sons. The eldest, Lachlan, was thirteen when I came to Camusfeàrna, and he had twin brothers of eleven, Ewan and Donald. The twins were eager, voluble, and helpful, by intention if not in every case in result, and after the first weeks, when the family had become my friends, it was they who would carry my mail down from Druimfiaclach in the evenings after school, and at week-ends do various odd jobs for me about the house. They painted the out-side walls of the house with Snowcem for me—or as much of the walls as their diminutive statures and a broken ladder could compass. They carried the heavy white powder down from Druimfiaclach in paper bags, and one day I suggested that they would find it easier to use my rucksack. They were delighted with the suggestion, and returned the following day with the whole rucksack full to the lip with loose Snowcem powder, and not only the main well of the rucksack but every zip-fastening pocket that the makers had designed for such personal possessions as toothbrushes and tobacco. That was nine years ago, and the twins are grown-up and out in the world, but in wet weather that rucksack still exudes a detectable whitish paste at the seams.

Gradually the MacKinnon household became my lifeline, my only link with the remote world of shops and post offices, of telegrams and anger, that I would so much have wished to dispense with altogether. It is not easy at any time to victual a house that has no road to it, and it becomes the more difficult when the nearest village with more than one shop is between thirty and forty miles distant by road. The mails themselves arrive at Druimfiaclach, once a day, by a complicated mixture of sea and road transport from the railhead at the shopping village. From it they are carried by motor-launch to a tiny village five miles from Druimfiaclach, where originally a vast old Humber and now a Land Rover takes over and distributes them among the scattered dwellings of the neighbourhood. I am, therefore, reasonably certain of receiving one post a day if I plod up the hill to Druimfiaclach to fetch it (though occasionally it is too rough for the launch to put out, and it is not unknown, this being the West Highlands, for the whole mailbag to be sent to Skye through oversight or petulance), but I can only leave a reply to that post at Druimfiaclach the following night, for collection by the Land Rover on the morning after that; so that if I receive a letter on, for example, a Tuesday evening, it will be Friday before the sender gets my reply. Newspapers reach me on the evening of the day after they are published, if I go to Druimfiaclach to fetch them. Because of the height of the surrounding mountain massifs no radio will emit more than a furtive whisper; by pressing one's ear to the set one may catch tantalizingly fragmentary snatches of news, too often of wars and rumours of wars, or of equally intrusive and unwelcome strains of rock 'n roll, mouse-squeak reminders of far-off human frenzy, whose faintness underlines the isolation of Camusfeàrna more effectively than could utter silence.

In practice, the exchange of letters often takes a full week, and the frustrations inherent in this situation have led the more impatient of my friends to the copious use of telegrams. The only way in which a telegram can be delivered, other than by the Land Rover carrying the mail to Druimfiaclach in the evenings, is by five steep and weary miles' bicycling from the Post Office to Druimfiaclach, followed by a mile and a half of hill-track on foot. In all, ten miles bicycling and three miles walking. The village postmaster is a man of extreme rectitude and sense of duty; the first telegram I ever received at Camusfeàrna was when on a sweltering summer's day, the hills shimmering in the heat haze and the fly-tormented cattle knee-deep in the motionless sea, he stood exhausted before my door bearing a message which read 'Many happy returns of the day'. The mountains had travailed and brought forth a mouse; after that I persuaded him, with great difficulty, to exercise his own judgment as to whether or not a telegram was urgent, and to consign those that were not to the Land Rover for delivery to Druimfiaclach in the evening.

Telegrams between the West Highlands and England are often liable to a little confusion in transit, to the production of what the services call 'corrupt groups'. During my first stay at Camusfeàrna I realized that though the house had, as it were, dropped into my lap from heaven, I had no subsidiary rights; a diet composed largely of shellfish might, I thought, be suitably varied by rabbits, and I telegraphed to the owner of the estate to ask his permission. The telegram he received from me read: 'May I please shoot at Robert and if so where?'

The reply to this sadistic request being in the affirmative, I shot at Robert morning and evening, with a silenced .22 from the kitchen window, and he went far to solve the supply problem both for myself and for my dog Jonnie. Alas, Robert and all his brothers have now gone from Camusfeàrna, and except by living entirely from the sea it is difficult to approach self-subsistence.

For a year or two there was goats' milk, for Morag had, characteristically, given asylum to four goats left homeless by their owner's demise; one of these, a dainty, frolicsome white sprite called Mairi Bhan, she presented to Camusfeàrna. It was but a token gesture, for the little nanny was unaware of any change in ownership, preferring the company of her co-concubines and her rancid, lecherous overlord. The herd, however, took to spending much of their time at Camusfeàrna, where they would pick their way delicately along the top of the croft wall to plunder and maim the old apple and plum trees by the bridge, necessitating strange high barriers that seem cryptic now, for the goats are long gone. Their cynical, predatory yellow eyes, bright with an ancient, egotistical wisdom, were ever alert for an open door, and more than once I came back to the house from an afternoon's fishing to find the kitchen in chaos, my last loaves disappearing between agile rubbery lips, and Mairi Bhan posturing impudently on the table.

In the end their predilection for Camusfeàrna was their undoing, for where a past occupier of the house had once grown a kitchen garden sprung rhubarb leaves in profusion; of these, one spring, they ate copiously, and all but the billy died. Never sweet to the nostrils or continent of habit, he became, deprived of his harem, so gross both in odour and in behaviour, that only the undeniable splendour of his appearance prevented my joining the

ranks of his numerous enemies. He survived, a lonely satyr, a sad solitary symbol of thwarted virility, until the burden of his chastity became too great for him, and he wandered and perished.

The goats were not the only invaders of the house, for in those days there was no fence surrounding it, and a door left ajar was taken as tacit invitation to the most improbable and unwelcome of visitors. Once, on my return to the house after a few hours' absence, I was warned of some crisis while as yet a quarter of a mile distant; a succession of mighty, hollow groans, interspersed with a sound as of one striking wooden boarding with a heavy mallet, conjured an image worse, if possible, than the bizarre reality. Half-way up the wooden stairway, where it turns at right angles to reach the small landing, an enormous, black, and strikingly pregnant cow was wedged fast between the two walls, unable to progress forward and fearful of the gradient in reverse. Her rear aspect, whose copious activity—whether under the stress of anxiety or from an intelligent desire to reduce her dimensions— covered the stairs below her with a positively Augean litter of dung, blocked both view and passage to any would-be rescuer; moreover she proved, despite her precarious foothold and elephantine fecundity, to be capable of kicking with a veritably faun-like flourish. It was, however, one of these moments of petulant aggression that brought, literally, her downfall; an attempt with both heels simultaneously collapsed her with a ponderous and pathetic rumble, and she lay on her great gravid belly with her legs trailing, mire-covered, down the stairs. When at the end of nearly an hour's haulage I had restored her to the outside world I feared for her calf, but I need not have worried. Not long after- wards I assisted at her delivery, not with forceps but with ropes attached to protruding hooves; the calf fell with a terrifying crash to a stone floor, and half an hour later was on his feet and suckling.

With the goats cut short, as I have said, in their connubial prime, Camusfeàrna has ever since been dependent upon tinned milk. General supplies reach me by the same three-stage route as the mail, with the assistance of the friendly, haphazard co-operation to be found in remote places. I leave my order for the grocer, the ironmonger, or the chemist at Druimfiaclach in the evening; the Land Rover collects it in the morning and hands it to the skipper of the mail launch, who delivers it to the shops and brings the goods back—if, that is, they are to be obtained at the 'shopping centre'. For though there are a surprising number of shops for what is really no more than a hamlet, there is also surprisingly little in them—the nearest place where such common-place objects as, for example, a coat-hanger or a pair of blue jeans may be bought, is Inverness, nearly a hundred miles away on the opposite coast of Scotland, or Fort William, the same distance to the south. This is not due entirely to a somewhat characteristic lack of enterprise, but also to a Foolish Virgin attitude to the necessities of life that I had seen exemplified again and again during my ownership of the Island of Soay. It is only during my own time at Camusfeàrna that electricity has come to the district —though not to me—through the West of Scotland Hydro-Electric Board; before that all the houses were lit by paraffin lamps, and many of the people cooked by Primus stove. Yet, despite the notoriously capricious quality of the electric light in the north-west Highlands, every single shop in every single village immediately stopped stocking paraffin, methylated spirits, and candles. Last year, there was to my certain knowledge, no drop of methylated spirits for sale within a hundred miles. The friendly spirit of co-operation is, however, equal even to this situation:

once I sent an S.O.S. for methylated spirits to a distant village and received an odd-looking package in return. It did not look like methylated spirits, and I unwrapped it in puzzlement. Inside was a pencil note which I deciphered with difficulty: 'Sorry no methylated spirits but am sending you two pounds of sausages instead.'

With a view to avoiding the monotony of tinned food I began early to experiment with edible fungi, but the results were not encouraging, and I have never succeeded in making them a substantial item of Camusfeàrna diet. I possessed two books, representing respectively and most decoratively the edible and harmful species; thus armed I set off one August day, the sun as hot as it can be upon rock lichen and bell heather, to collect and identify all I could. At evening I returned laden with, it appeared, considerably more varieties than existed in both books put together. With these arranged like a palette of pastel shades upon the kitchen table, and both slim volumes at hand for consultation, I began eagerly to separate the sheep from the goats. Almost at once, however, I discovered that every edible species had a poisonous counterpart whose uniform was so exactly similar as to defy detection. At the end of half an hour I gathered friend and masquerading enemy indiscriminately together and bundled them into the refuse pit. Now there is only one fungus that I find worth the trouble of search, the *Boletus edulis*, that has a glazed brown top like a bun, and tastes strongly of mushroom. The *chanterelles*, delicate orange creatures shaped like toy trumpets, grow in enormous profusion under the trees about the hill-side burns, but though an eighteenth-century writer said of them that dead men would come to life at the taste, I have found them flavourless and insipid, their beauty but skin-deep, more appropriate to the magic of moss and fern and rushing water than to the table.

As children the members of my family were brought up to regard fungi with a conservative eye, and though we gathered and consumed vast quantities of horse mushrooms, we were taught to believe that puffballs were poisonous. More recently I have learned that they are not, but how they have won the gourmet's esteem remains to me a marvel; they are the most non-committal, self-effacing food I have ever eaten, tasting of nothing and being of no definable consistency, gastronomic nonentities *par excellence*. Sometimes I wonder whether their adulators have ever tasted them; Miss Rowena Farre ate them in *Seal Morning*, if one may put it that way, and found them delicious.

So the fungi at Camusfeàrna remain, for the most part, un-molested, and flourish among the ferns and dappled sunlight of the birches by the burns and the hidden waterfalls, their many hues of violet and green, red and orange, nibbled at by discerning and appreciative rodents whose perceptions are undimmed by attempted identification of their diet.

3

I HAD been at Camusfeàrna for eight years before I piped water to the house; before that it came from the burn in buckets. During the first years there was a stout stone-piered bridge across the burn, and under it one could draw water that had not been fouled by the cattle at their ford a little lower; then, in 1953, the bridge was swept away by a winter spate, and there was none built again for five years. In the summer there is no more than a foot or so of water among the stones, deepening to three or four feet when it runs amber-coloured and seemingly motionless between the alder banks, but wedged high among the branches are wads of debris that show the level of its torrential winter spates. When the gales blow in from the south-west and the burn comes roaring down in a foaming peaty cataract to meet the invading sea, the alders stand under water for half their height, and in the summer blackened trailers of dry seaweed dangle from branches ten feet and more above the stream.

After the bridge had gone, the winter crossing of the burn to climb the hill to Druimfiaclach was always perilous, sometimes impossible. I stretched a rope between the alders from bank to bank, but it was slender support, for even when the water was no more than thigh deep the pure battering weight of it as it surged down from the waterfall would sweep one's legs from the bottom and leave one clinging to the rope without foothold, feet trailing seaward.

The purely natural changes that have taken place during my ten years at Camusfeàrna are astonishing. One is inclined to think of such a landscape as immutable without the intervention of man, yet in these few years the small alterations to the scene have been continuous and progressive. The burn has swept the soil from under its banks so that the alder roots show white and bare, and some of the trees have fallen; where there are none at the burn side the short green turf has been tunnelled under by the water so that it falls in and the stream's bed becomes ever wider and shallower. Farther down towards the sea, where the burn bends round to encircle Camusfeàrna, the burrowing of a colony of sand martins in the sand cliff that is its landward bank has had the same effect, undermining the turf above so that it gives beneath the sheeps' feet and rolls down to the water's edge. Below the sand martins' burrows is now a steep slope of loose sand where ten years ago it was vertical. The sand dunes between the house and the sea form and re-form, so that their contour is never the same for two years, though the glaucous, rasping marram grass that grows on them imparts an air of static permanency. The whole structure of these dunes that now effectively block much of the beach from the house, and incidentally afford to it some shelter from the southerly gales, is in any case a thing of recent times, for I am told that when the present house was built fifty-odd years ago the field stretched flat to the sea, and the seaward facing wall of the house was left windowless for that reason.

The beach itself, wherever the rock does not shelve straight into the sea, is in constant change too; broad belts of shingle appear in the sand where there was no shingle before; soft stretches of quicksand come and go in a few weeks; sand bars as white as snow-drifts and jewelled with bright shells rise between the islands and vanish as though they had melted under the summer suns.

Even the waterfall, to me perhaps the most enduring symbol of Camusfeàrna, has changed and goes on changing. When I am away from the place and think of it, it is of the waterfall that I think first. Its voice is in one's ears day and night; one falls asleep to it, dreams with it and wakens to it; the note changes with the season, from the dull menacing roar of winter nights to the low crooning of the summer, and if I hold a shell to my ear it is not the sea's murmur that comes to me but the sound of the Camus-feàrna waterfall. Above the bridge where I used to draw my water the burn rushes over stones and between boulders with the alders at its banks, and a wealth of primroses and wild hyacinths among the fern and mosses. In spring it is loud with bird song from the chaffinches that build their lichen nests in the forks of the alders, and abob with wagtails among the stones. This part of the burn is 'pretty' rather than beautiful, and it seems to come from nowhere, for the waterfall is hidden round a corner and the stream seems to emerge from a thirty-foot wall of rock hung with honey-suckle and with rowan trees jutting from cracks and fissures. But looking up the burn from the foot of that rock the word 'pretty' becomes wholly inapplicable; the waterfall is of a beauty it would be hard to devise. It is not high, for the tall cataracts of eighty feet are some two hundred yards higher up its course; it emerges between boulders and sheer rock walls to drop some fifteen feet, over about the same breadth, from the twilight world of the deep narrow gorge it has carved through the hill face over thousands, perhaps millions, of years. It emerges frothing from that unseen darkness to fall like a tumbling cascade of brilliants into a deep rounded cauldron enclosed by rock walls on three sides, black water in whorled black rock, with the fleecy white spume ringing the blackness of the pool. Up above the black sides of the pot there are dark-green watery mosses growing deep and cushioned wherever there is a finger-hold for soil; the domed nest that the dippers build here every year is distinguishable from the other moss cushions by nothing but its symmetry. The sun reaches the waterfall for only a short time in the afternoon; it forms a rainbow over the leaping spray, and at the top of the fall between the boulders it gives to the smooth-flowing, unbroken water the look of spun green glass.

For most of the year the waterfall has volume enough for a man to stand on a ledge between it and the rock and remain almost dry; between oneself and the sky it forms a rushing, deafening curtain of milky brilliance through which nothing but light is discernible. If one steps forward so that the weight of water batters full on head and shoulders it is of the massiveness only that one is conscious, and it would be impossible to say whether the water were cold or hot. Only when one steps from it again, and the flying icy drops tingle on the skin, does the sensation become one of snow water.

It would seem that the waterfall could never change, yet year by year its form differs as a new boulder is swept down by the spates to lodge above its lip; or a tree falls from its precarious grip on the cliff faces above it and jams the doorway of its emergence; or a massive section of rock breaks away, split by the prising leverage of slow-growing tree roots.

In spring and autumn the natural decoration surrounding the waterfall surpasses anything that artifice could achieve; in spring the green banks above the rock are set so thickly with primroses that blossom almost touches blossom, and the wild blue hyacinths spring from among them seemingly without leaf; in late summer and autumn the scarlet rowanberries flare from the ferned rock walls, bright against the falling white water and the darkness of the rock.

It is the waterfall, rather than the house, that has always seemed to me the soul of Camusfeàrna, and if there is anywhere in the world to which some part of me may return when I am dead it will be there.

If it is the waterfall that seems the soul of Camusfeàrna, it is the burn and the sea that give its essential character, that sparkling silver that rings the green field and makes it almost an island. Below the house the beach is long and shelving, the tide running back at low springs for more than two hundred yards over alternate stone and sand. There is only one thing lacking at Camusfeàrna; within its narrow compass it contains every attraction but an anchorage. To look down from the hill above upon the bay and the scattered, intricate network of islands and skerries it would appear incredible that no one of those bights or niches should afford shelter, yet because of the long ebb of the tide each one of these seemingly tranquil miniature harbours dries out at low water. For years I had no boat at Camusfeàrna, and when at last I did buy a dinghy I was intimidated by the thought of those interminable hauls to and from the water's edge, and I bought a little nine-foot flat-bottomed pram that one could almost pick up. But to have a boat again at all, even that toy, brought a hankering to extend one's range up and down the coast and over to Skye, and now I have two dinghies with outboard motors, one of them a sturdy lifeboat's dinghy of fifteen feet, with decked-in bows. There are moorings laid in the bay where the burn flows out to the sea, and the pram is kept drawn up on the beach as ferry to and from the larger boat, but when the wind blows strong from the south it is always an anxious business. The suddenness and intensity of West Highland squalls, even in summer, has to be experienced to be understood; pale-blue satin water can become in a matter of minutes an iron-grey menace raging in white at the crests of massive waves. But the compensations outweigh the anxiety, for it was frustrating to live at the sea's edge and be unable to voyage upon it, to be unable to visit the distant islands, to fish in summer, to reach the nearest shop without the long climb to Druimfiaclach. The possession of the boats opened a whole new world around Camusfeàrna, a wide extension of its small enclosed paradise, and in summer the hours afloat drift by with work unheeded and the business of life seeming far off and worthless.

There is a perpetual mystery and excitement in living on the seashore, which is in part a return to childhood and in part because for all of us the sea's edge remains the edge of the unknown; the child sees the bright shells, the vivid weeds and red sea-anemones of the rock pools with wonder and with the child's eye for minutiae; the adult who retains wonder brings to his gaze some partial knowledge which can but increase it, and he brings, too, the eye of association and of symbolism, so that at the edge of the ocean he stands at the brink of his own unconscious.

The beaches of Camusfeàrna are a treasure house for any man whose eye finds wealth at the sea's edge. There are more shells than I have seen on any other littoral; a great host of painted bivalves of bewildering variety and hue, from coral pinks and primrose yellows to blues and purples and mother-of-pearl, from jewel-like fan shells no bigger than a little fingernail to the great scallops as big as a side-plate; nutshells and Hebridean ark shells and pearly top-shells and delicate blush-pink cowries. The sandbars and beaches between the islands are formed of the disintegration of these myriad calceous houses, true shell sand that is blindingly white under the sun and crusted in deep layers at the tide's edge with tiny intact empty shells gaudy as multi-coloured china beads. A little above the shells, because they are heavier, lies a filigree of white and purple coral, loose pieces each of which would lie in the palm of a hand, but there are so many of them that they form a dense, brittle layer over the sand. On still summer days when the tide wells up the beaches without so much as a wrinkle or ripple of wavelet at its edge, the coral floats off on the maniscus of the water, so that the sea seems to be growing flowers as an ornamental pond grows water lilies, delicately branched white and purple flowers on the aquamarine of the clear water.

Where shells lie thick it is often those that are broken that have the greatest beauty of form; a whelk is dull until one may see the sculptural perfection of the revealed spiral, the skeletal intricacy of the whorled mantle. Many of the shells at Camusfeàrna, and the stones, too, have been embroidered with the white limy tunnels of the serpulid tube-worm, strange hieroglyphics that even in their simplest forms may appear urgently significant, the symbols of some forgotten alphabet, and when a surface is thickly encrusted it assumes the appearance of Hindoo temple carving, or of Rodin's Gates of Hell, precise in every riotous ramification. Parts of the sculpture appear almost representational; a terrified beast flees before a pursuing predator; a well-meaning saint impales a dragon; the fingers of a hand are raised, like those of a Byzantine Christ, in a gesture that seems one of negation rather than benediction.

But above all it is the fantastic colouring of the beaches that as an image overpowers the minutiae. Above the tide-line the grey rocks are splashed gorse-yellow with close-growing lichen, and with others of blue-green and salmon pink. Beneath them are the vivid orange-browns and siennas of wrack-weeds, the violet of mussel-beds, dead-white sand, and water through which one sees down to the bottom, as through pale green bottle-glass, to where starfish and big spiny sea urchins of pink and purple rest upon the broad leaves of the sea-tangle.

The beaches are rich, too, in edible shellfish. Besides the ubiquitous mussels, limpets and periwinkles, there are cockle beds, razor-shell beds, and even an oyster bed, though this last remains one of the mysteries of Camusfeàrna. The oysters were introduced many years ago by a former owner of the estate, in a little circular bay almost closed from the sea and no more than twenty yards across, where a trickle of fresh water comes down over the sand from an island spring. At the tideline above this bay arrives a constant litter of tantalizingly freshly emptied oyster shells that would not disgrace Wheeler's, and, very occasionally, a live oyster, but for all my searching year by year I have never discovered where the bed lies. This is as well, perhaps, for I suspect that by now the colony would have succumbed to my gluttony.

Below the tide around the islands the white sand alternates with a heavy rubbery jungle of sea-tangle or umbrella weed. The lobsters lurk in this dimness by day, and lobster-pots set in the sand patches between the weed are rarely unsuccessful. A variety of other life besides lobsters enters the pots, creatures couth and uncouth; sometimes the bait is covered with gigantic whelks, and almost always there are big edible crabs. Often there is a curious beast called the velvet swimming crab, with a shield of brown velvet and reproachful red eyes, and once I caught one of the most repulsive creatures I have ever come across, a spider crab. It was not only the enormously long legs and absence of pincers that were nauseating; he was grown over from head to foot, as it were, with a crinkly, purplish-red seaweed, lending him the same air of doubtful reality as a shroud traditionally imparts to a ghost. The weed is, in fact, grafted into position by the crab itself, for camouflage, and this implication of furtive cunning coming on top of the outrageous personal appearance is not reassuring.

47

I must confess to a slight but perceptible revulsion to all crabs before they are prepared for eating, greatest in the case of the spider crab and in *diminuendo* down to the hermit-crabs that inhabit empty shells, for their unattractive nakedness is decently covered in someone else's discarded finery. Hermit crabs have given rise to some of the few occasions in my adult life on which I have laughed out loud when quite alone. Sometimes when gathering periwinkles to eat, bucket in hand and scooping them several dozen to a swipe, my attention has been caught by some monster winkle at the floor of a pool, one that would at least provide a mouthful for a marmoset rather than a mouse. Even as my fingers have broken the surface of the water, shaping themselves avidly for capture, the shell, its bluff so accidentally called, has suddenly scuttled away with an air of chagrin and embarrassment, as though two of the Marx brothers, detected in the front and rear halves of a stage cow, still made a last hopeless effort to maintain the deception.

4

SPRING COMES late to Camusfeàrna. More than one year I have motored up from the south early in April to become immobilized in snowdrifts on the passes twenty miles from it, and by then the stags are still at the roadside down the long glen that leads to the sea. By mid-April there is still no tinge of green bud on the bare birches and rowans nor green underfoot, though there is often, as when I first came to Camusfeàrna, a spell of soft still weather and clear skies. The colours then are predominantly pale blues, russet browns, and purples, each with the clarity of fine enamel; pale blue of sea and sky, the russet of dead bracken and fern, deep purple-brown of unbudded birch, and the paler violets of the Skye hills and the peaks of Rhum. The landscape is lit by three whites—the pearl white of the birch trunks, the dazzle of the shell-sand beaches, and the soft filtered white of the high snows. The primroses are beginning to flower about the burn and among the island banks, though all the high hills are snow-covered and the lambs are as yet unborn. It is a time that has brought me, in all too few years, the deep contentment of knowing that the true spring and summer are still before me at Camusfeàrna, that I shall see the leaf break and the ground become green, and all the snow melt from the hills but for a few drifts that will lie summer through.

49

It has its own orchestration, this little prelude to the northern spring; every year there is the sound of the wild geese calling far overhead as they travel north to their thawing breeding grounds, and sometimes the wild unearthly beauty of whooper swans' voices, silver trumpets high in the clear blue air. The eider ducks have arrived to breed about the shore and the islands; they bring with them that most evocative and haunting of all sounds of the Hebridean spring and summer, the deep, echoing, wood-wind crooning of the courting drakes.

One by one the breeding bird species return to the beaches and the islands where they were hatched; the sand martins to the sand cliff at the burn foot, the wheatears to the rabbit burrows in the close-bitten turf, the black guillemots and the gulls to the Camus-feàrna islands. The herring gulls come first, to the biggest island, where the lighthouse stands, some two hundred and fifty pairs of them, and the air above the white-splashed rocks and sea pinks scattered with broken shellfish is vibrant with the clang of their calling and their wheeling white wings. Among them are two or three pairs of great black-backed gulls, massive, hoarse-voiced and vulturine. Then come the common gulls, delicate, graceful, segregated shrilly on to a neighbouring promontory, beadily mistrustful of the coarse language and predatory predilections of their neighbours; and, lastly, not until well into May, come the terns, the sea-swallows, to their own outlying skerry. They arrive in the same week as the swallows come up from Africa to nest in the old ruined croft across the field, and with the thin steel oar-beat of their wings spring has almost given place to summer.

By then the colour everywhere is green. The purple birch twigs are hidden in a soft cloud of new leaf; the curled, almond-bitter rods of young bracken have in those short weeks pushed up three feet from the earth and unfurled a canopy of green frond over the rust of last year's growth; the leaves of the yellow flag iris that margin the burn and the shore form a forest of broad bayonets, and the islands, that but for rank rooty patches of heather growing knee-deep seemed so bare in April, are smothered with a jungle-growth of goose grass and briar. To me there is always something a little stifling in this enveloping green stain, this redundant, almost Victorian, drapery over bones that need no blanketing, and were it not for the astringent presence of the sea I should find all that verdure as enervating as an Oxford water-meadow in the depths of summer. Perhaps 'depraved' is the right word after all.

Early in May comes the recurrent miracle of the elvers' migration from the sea. There is something deeply awe-inspiring about the sight of any living creatures in incomputable numbers; it stirs, perhaps, some atavistic chord whose note belongs more properly to the distant days when we were a true part of the animal ecology; when the sight of another species in unthinkable hosts brought fears or hopes no longer applicable. When the young eels reach the Camusfeàrna burn—no more than a uniform three inches long nor thicker than a meat-skewer, steel-blue when seen from above, but against the light transparent except for a red blob at the gills—they have been journeying in larval form for two whole years from their breeding grounds south-west of Bermuda, through two thousand miles of ocean and enemies. During that long, blind voyage of instinct their numbers must have been reduced not to a millionth but a billionth of those who set forth, yet it is difficult to imagine that there can have been vaster hoards than reach the Camusfeàrna burn; still more difficult to realize that these are but a tiny fraction of the hosts that are simultaneously ascending a myriad other burns.

Where the burn flows calm through the level ground their armies undulate slowly and purposefully forward towards the seemingly insurmountable barrier of the falls; on, above the bridge, into the stretch where the water rushes and stumbles over uneven stones; round the rock-twist to the foot of the falls. Here, temporarily daunted or resting before their assault upon the vertical, spray-wet rock-face, they congregate almost motionless in the rock pools, forming a steel-blue carpet inches deep; dip a bucket here, and it comes up with a greater volume of elvers than of water. Some mistake the true course of the burn, and follow steep trickles leading to *cul-de-sac* pools of spray water; to and from these (for the miraculous powers of their multitudes do not appear to include communication or deduction), there are simultaneous streams of ascending and descending elvers, while the spray-pool itself is filled to the brim with an aimlessly writhing swarm.

It is here, during the wait at the foot of the falls, that the last heavy toll is taken of their numbers; for a week or two the rocks below the waterfall are splashed white with the droppings of herons who stand there scooping them up by the bill-full, decimating yet again, on the verge of their destination, the remnants of the great concourse that has been travelling thus perilously for two years.

But one has not been witness to the long core, as it were, of that mighty migration, and so it is in the elvers' final ascent of the falls that the colossal driving power of their instinct becomes most apparent to the onlooker. At first, where at the edges of the falls the water splashes into shallow stone troughs among the horizontal ledges, the way is easy—a few inches of horizontal climb and the elver has reached the next trough. But after a foot or two of this ladder-like progression they are faced either with the battering fall of white water at their left or with a smooth black stretch of rock wall in front, hit every few seconds by heavy splashes of spray. For a few feet at the bottom of this wall grows a close slimy fur of waterweed, and among its infinitesimal tendrils the elvers twine themselves and begin, very slowly, to squirm their way upwards, forming a vertical, close-packed queue perhaps two feet wide. Sometimes a big gob of spray lands right amid their ranks and knocks a hundred of them back into the trough below, but slowly, patiently, they climb back again. I have never marked an elver so that it is recognizable, and for all I know this may happen to the same elver many, many times in a day or even in an hour. Perhaps it is something to do with the transparency of the creatures, besides their diminutive size and bewildering numbers, that makes the mind rebel both at the blind strength of

The dinghy near to Camusfeàrna

Camusfeàrna

Jonnie above Camusfeàrna

The kitchen-living-room of Camusfeàrna in the early days

The waterfall in summer

Sand ribs at tide's edge

Shells decorated by the Serpulid tube worm

'Strange hieroglyphics that even in their simplest
forms may appear urgently significant'

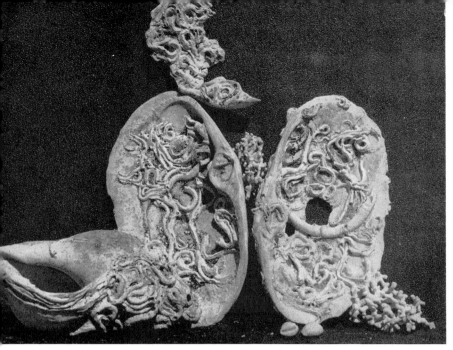

'The appearance of Hindoo temple carving, or of Rodin's
"Gates of Hell", precise in every riotous ramification'

Sea-worn wood

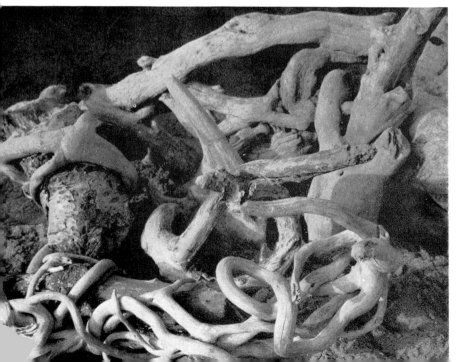

Storm and spume

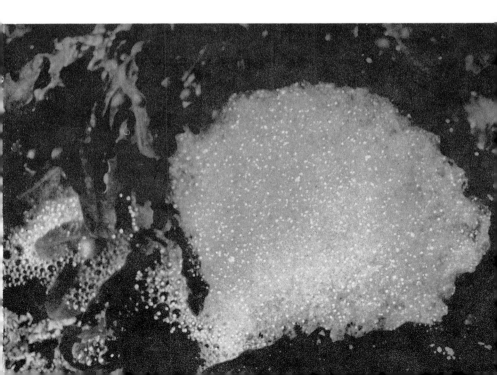

South of Camusfeàrna

Stag by the waterfall

Ptarmigan on the high tops

Migrating elvers climbing vertical rock at the falls' side

'dip a bucket here and it comes up with a greater volume of elvers than of water'. Elvers and eel-slime, technically known as 'vomp'

A bay near Camusfeàrna

Migrating Greylag geese

Whooper swans

'The eider ducks have arrived to breed about the shore and the islands'

Migrating White-fronted geese pass overhead

their instinct and their inherent power to implement it, as though the secret power-house should be visible.

Once above the water-draggled weed there is no further incidental support for the climbing elvers; there is just sheer wet rock, with whatever microscopic roughness their transparent bellies may apprehend. They hang there, apparently without gravity, with an occasional convulsive movement that seems born of despair. They climb perhaps six inches in an hour, sometimes slithering backward the same distance in a second, and there are a further twelve feet of rock above them.

It is not possible for more than a moment or two to identify oneself with any single one of this mass, but there is a sense of relief, of emotional satisfaction, in looking upward to the lip of the falls where they spill over from the hidden pool above, and seeing the broad band of glistening elvers that have accomplished the apparently impossible and are within an inch of safety.

Perhaps a few million out of billions top the Camusfeàrna falls; some, certainly, surmount the second and third falls too, and I have seen elvers of that size more than two thousand feet up the peak where the burn has its source. In perspective, the survival rate must be high when compared with that of spermatozoa.

Only once at Camusfeàrna have I seen any other living creatures in numbers to compare with those elvers, but I remember the occasion vividly. In the warm evenings of later summer, when the sun still flared a finger's breadth above the saw-tooth peaks of the Cuillin and glowed on the dense red berries of the rowans, the MacKinnon children would come down the hill from Druim-fiaclach to bathe at the white sand beaches of the islands. Long before I could hear them my dog Jonnie, growing a little corpulent and stiff now, would prick his ears and whine, and the feathery white stub of his tail would scuff softly on the stone floor. I would go to the open door and listen and Jonnie would sit very upright on the stone flags outside, staring up at the high skyline with his nose twitching and questing, and I would hear nothing but the sounds of ever-moving water and the faint, familiar bird-cries of the wilderness, the piping of shore birds and perhaps the mew of a buzzard wheeling overhead. There was the murmur of the dwindled waterfall and the trill of the burn among the boulders, and at the other side the muted sound of wavelets breaking in a small tumble of foam along the shore; there was the twitter of sand martins hawking flies in the still golden air, the croak of a raven, and gull voices from the sea that stretched away as smooth as white silk to the distant island of Eigg lying across the sea horizon. Sometimes there was the warning thump of a rabbit from the warren among the dunes behind the house.

But Jonnie always knew when the children were coming, and when at last I could hear them too, treble voices faint and far off and high above us, he would assume a sudden unconcern, walking with stiff indifference to lift his leg in a flourish over a nearby tuft of rushes or a post that guarded the small flower-bed. From the time that the boys' heads were bobbing small on the hill horizon it would be some five minutes before they had descended the last and steepest part of the track, crossed the bridge, and come up over the green grass to the door, and all the time I would be wondering what they had brought—longed-for or unwelcome letters, some supplies that I urgently needed, a bottle of goat's milk from their mother, or just nothing at all. When it was nothing I was at once relieved and bitterly disappointed, for at Camus-feàrna I both resent the intrusion of the outside world and crave reassurance of its continued existence.

One evening when the twins had brought me a bulky packet of letters I had been sitting reading them in the twilight kitchen for some time when I was roused by the urgent excitement of their cries from the beach. I went out to a scene that is as fresh in my mind now as though it were hours rather than years that lay between.

The sun was very low; the shadow of the house lay long and

dark across the grass and the rushes, while the hill-side above glowed golden as though seen through orange lenses. The bracken no longer looked green nor the heather purple; all that gave back their own colour to the sun were the scarlet rowanberries, as vivid as venous blood. When I turned to the sea it was so pale and polished that the figures of the twins thigh-deep in the shallows showed in almost pure silhouette against it, bronze-coloured limbs and torsos edged with yellow light. They were shouting and laughing and dancing and scooping up the water with their hands, and all the time as they moved there shot up from the surface where they broke it a glittering spray of small gold and silver fish, so dense and brilliant as to blur the outline of the childish figures. It was as though the boys were the central dècor of a strangely lit Baroque fountain, and when they bent to the surface with cupped hands a new jet of sparks flew upward where their arms submerged, and fell back in brittle, dazzling cascade.

When I reached the water myself it was like wading in silver treacle; our bare legs pushed against the packed mass of little fish as against a solid and reluctantly yielding obstacle. To scoop and to scatter them, to shout and to laugh, were as irresistible as though we were treasure hunters of old who had stumbled upon a fabled emperor's jewel vaults and threw diamonds about us like chaff. We were fish-drunk, fish-crazy, fish-happy in that shining orange bubble of air and water; the twins were about thirteen years old and I was about thirty-eight, but the miracle of the fishes drew from each of us the same response.

We were so absorbed in making the thronged millions of tiny fish into leaping fireworks for our delight that it was not for some minutes that I began to wonder what had driven this titanic shoal of herring fry—or soil, as they are called in this part of the world —into the bay, and why, instead of dispersing outwards to sea, they became moment by moment ever thicker in the shallows. Then I saw that a hundred yards out the surface was ruffled by flurries of mackerel whose darting shoals made a sputter of spray on the smooth swell of the incoming tide. The mackerel had driven the fry headlong before them into the narrow bay and held them there, but now the pursuers too were unable to go back. They were in turn harried from seaward by a school of porpoises who cruised the outermost limit of their shoals, driving them farther and farther towards the shore. Hunter and hunted pushed the herring soil ever inward to the sand, and at length every wavelet broke on the beach with a tumble of silver sprats. I wondered that the porpoises had not long since glutted and gone; then I saw that, like the fry and the mackerel that had pursued them into the bay, the porpoises' return to the open waters of the sound was cut off. Beyond them, black against the blanched sunset water, rose the towering sabre fin of a bull killer whale, the ultimate enemy of sea creatures great and small, the unattackable; his single terrible form controlling by its mere presence the billions of lives between himself and the shore.

The sun went down behind the Cuillin and the water grew cold and the tide crawled grey up the beach, clogged with its helpless burden of fish, and long after the distance had become too dim to see the killer's fin we could hear the putter of the rushing mackerel as they moved in with the tide. When it was nearly dark we fetched buckets and dipped them in the sea's edge; they came up heavy in our hands, full not of water but of thumb-length fish.

In the morning it was dead low tide, and the sea, as still as a mountain tarn as far as the eye could reach, had gone back some two hundred yards. The tide-wrack of high-water mark lay right along the slope of white sand under the dunes, but that morning it was not dark like a tarry rope ringing the bay; it gleamed blue-grey and white with the bodies of millions upon millions of motionless minnow-sized fish. The gulls had gorged themselves when the sun rose; they sat silent, hunched and distended, in long rows on the wet sand a little to seaward, their shadows still long and formal under the low sun that glared over the hill.

I gathered a few more buckets of the fry, and kept them as cool as I could in the heat of that sunny September. But manna, like everything else, should be of at least fifty-seven varieties; when heaven sends bounty it too often sends monotony. The first meal of fried whitebait had the delight of novelty and of windfall, akin to the pleasure that for the first few days I take in some humble but new treasure harvested from the shore after gales; the second had lost little, but the sixth and seventh were cloying, while there were still three buckets full. Jonnie, who entertained an unnatural passion for fish of all kinds, ate more than I did, but the level in the buckets seemed never to diminish; a guest came to stay, and we made them into fish-cakes and fish-pies, into kedgerees and fish-soups, into curries and savouries, until at last one merciful morning they began to smell. Then we used them to bait the lobster-pots, but after a while even the lobsters seemed to grow weary of them.

It so happened that about that time I made one of my rare shopping journeys to Inverness. The second item on the hotel luncheon menu was fried whitebait, and the dining-room was rich with the once-appetizing aroma. I left that hotel as might one who had perceived a corpse beneath his table, and it was some two years before I could eat whitebait again.

5

THE SMALLER members of the whale tribe are a feature of every summer at Camusfeàrna. Sometimes the great whales, the Blue and the Rorquals, pass majestically through the Sound beyond the lighthouse, but they never come into the bay, for only at the highest of tides would there be water enough to float their fantastic bulk.

Of all sea creatures whales hold for me a particular fascination, stemming, perhaps, from the knowledge of their enormously developed brains coupled with the unguessable, pressing, muffled world in which they pass their lives. So highly convoluted are those brains that it has been suggested that were it not for their frustrating limbless-ness they might well have outstripped man in domination of the earth's surface. Yet there are an incredible number of people who, because of the superficial similarities of bulk and habitat, confuse them with the great sharks whose brains are minute and rudimentary. Although from early times whaling men have had strange tales to tell of their quarry's extraordinary mental powers it is only comparatively recently that these things have become accepted fact. The American 'oceanariums' have allowed their porpoise and dolphin inmates to reveal themselves as highly intelligent, amiable, and playful personalities who evince an unexpected desire to please and co-operate with human beings. They will play ball games with their attendants, come up out of the water to greet them, and retrieve with obvious pleasure ladies' handbags and kindred objects that have accidentally fallen into their tank. They are also capable of unquestionable altruism to one another; like many animals, but perhaps even more than most, their behaviour compares very favourably with that of the human species. Yet for the oil in the blubber that insulates them from the cold of polar seas man has from the earliest days reserved for the whales the most brutal and agonizing death in his armoury, the harpoon buried deep in living flesh.

Until very lately zoologists held that whales were dumb, and both the system of communication that made possible concerted action by widely separated individuals, and the 'sixth sense' by which they could detect the presence of objects in water too murky for vision, remained undiscovered. We have long laboured under an obtuse presupposition that the senses by which other living creatures perceive their world must to a great extent resemble our own; but in fact we are, by scientific invention, only now beginning to approach methods of perception that the whales have always owned as their birthright. Not only can they hear sounds four times higher than the upper limit the human ear can detect, but they possess a highly-developed system closely akin to our own recently discovered radar, sending out a constant stream of supersonic notes whose returning 'echoes' inform them of the whereabouts, size, and possibly much more as yet unguessed information, of all objects within their range. Underwater recording devices have now also established that members of the whale tribe keep up an almost continual conversational chatter among themselves, sounds that are seldom if ever uttered by a single whale with no other near him.

Because man could not hear them, man assumed that they were dumb. If a whale's cry of pain when struck with a harpoon had been audible it is just possible, but only just, that man would have felt more self-hatred in their slaughter; though the sight of two adult whales trying to keep the blow-hole of a wounded calf above water has failed to change the attitude of whaler to whale.

It is not, of course, easy for the casual shore visitor or boat passenger to deduce from the discreet, momentarily-glimpsed fin of a porpoise all these complex and stimulating attributes of its owner; surprisingly few people, in fact, appear even to know that a porpoise is a whale.

The porpoises, six-foot lengths of sturdy grace, are the commonest of all the whale visitors to the Camusfeàrna bay. Unlike the rumbustious dolphins they are shy, retiring creatures, and one requires leisure and patience to see more of them than that little hooked fin that looks as if it were set on the circumference of a slowly-revolving wheel; leisure to ship the oars and remain motionless, and patience to allow curiosity to overcome timidity. Then the porpoises will blow right alongside the boat, with a little gasp that seems of shocked surprise, and at these close quarters the wondering inquisitiveness of their eyes shows as plainly as it can in a human face, a child's face as yet uninhibited against the display of emotion. The face, like the faces of all whales but the killer, appears good-humoured, even bonhomous. But they will not stay to be stared at, and after that quick gasp they dive steeply down into the twilight; they go on about their own business, and will not linger to play as do the dolphins.

One summer a school of seventeen Bottle-nosed dolphins spent a whole week in the Camusfeàrna bay, and they would seem almost to hang about waiting for the boat to come out and play with them. They never leapt and sported unless the human audience was close at hand, but when we were out among them with the outboard motor they would play their own rollicking and hilarious games of hide-and-seek with us, and a sort of aquatic blind-man's-buff, in which we in the boat were all too literally blind to them, and a target for whatever surprises they could devise. The beginning followed an invariable routine; they would lead, close-packed, their fins thrusting from the water with a long powerful forward surge every five or ten seconds, and we would follow to see how close we could get to them. When we were within fifty feet or so there would be a sudden silence while, unseen, they swooped back under the boat to reappear dead astern of us. Sometimes they would remain submerged for many minutes, and we would cut the engine and wait. This was the dolphins' moment. As long as I live, and whatever splendid sights I have yet to see I shall remember the pure glory of the dolphins' leap as they shot up a clear ten feet out of the sea, one after the other, in high parabolas of flashing silver at the very boat's side. At the time it gave me a *déjà-vu* sensation that I could not place; afterwards I realized that it recalled irresistibly the firing in quick succession of pyrotechnic rockets, the tearing sound of the rockets' discharge duplicated by the harsh exhalation of air as each dolphin fired itself almost vertically from the waves.

In this school of dolphins there were some half a dozen calves, not more than four or five feet long as against their parents' twelve. The calves would keep close alongside their mothers' flanks—the right-hand side always—and I noticed that when the mothers leapt they kept their acrobatics strictly within the capabilities of their offspring, rising no more than half the height of those unencumbered by children.

The members of this school of dolphins spoke with voices perfectly audible to human ears; rarely when they were very close to the boat, but usually when they were heading straight away at a distance of a hundred yards or two. As they broke the surface with that strong forward-thrusting movement, one or more of their number would produce something between a shrill whistle and a squeak, on a single note held for perhaps two seconds. It seems strange that I can find no written record of any whale-sound as plainly and even obtrusively audible above water as this.

The Risso's Grampus, or more properly Risso's Dolphin, a few feet larger than the Bottle-nose, visits Camusfeàrna bay in the summer too, but whereas in the shark fishery days I used to regard them as the sea's clowns, perpetually at play in uncouth and incongruous attitudes, the parties that come to Camusfeàrna have by comparison with the Bottle-nosed been sedate and decorous, almost always cows with small tubby calves, intent on the serious business of feeding and avoiding danger. They would not allow the boat nearly as close to them as would the other dolphins, unlike whom they seemed to resent human presence, and would soon leave the bay altogether if frequently followed.

Contrary to information contained in the majority of textbooks, in which Risso's dolphin is described as a rarity, it is in fact the commonest of all the lesser whales to visit the Hebrides in summer. During my years in the shark fishery, when our chief catcher the *Sea Leopard* would cruise day-long in search of a different shape of fin, it was a rare week in which we had not met with half a dozen schools of them. As with most other species of whale, the fishermen have their own names for them, names that they sometimes, to the confusion of an enquiring scientist, use to describe several separate species, so that it is only by the comparatively very rare strandings of individual whales that the presence of a species becomes established. The ring-net men call Risso's dolphin 'lowpers' or 'dunters', words deriving from the habit of seemingly aimless and random leaping. Neither Risso's nor the Bottle-nosed dolphins travel, as do the white-sided and common dolphins, by a series of long leaps low over the waves; both seem to jump only when they are at leisure and frolicking.

In fact it is not easy for an eye with any practice to confuse the fin of Risso's dolphin with any other than that of a cow Killer whale. 'Cow' is a strange feminine noun to give to the most terrible animal in the sea; 'bull' is little better for her butcher mate, but the forms are fixed by long usage and must stand. Imaginations have strained to find a simile from land animals; the Killer has been called the wolf of the sea, the tiger of the sea, the hyena of the sea, but none of these is really apt, and probably there is no other mammal of comparably indiscriminate ferocity.

Anyone writing of Killer whales finds it necessary to quote the discovered contents of one Killer's stomach, and indeed those contents produce so immediate an image that they will, perhaps, bear one more repetition. That particular Killer was found to contain no fewer than thirteen porpoises and fourteen seals. A gargantuan meal, one would say, for a leviathan, yet by comparison with the great whales the Killer is a small beast, the bull no more than twenty-five feet overall and the cow a mere fifteen, while an adult porpoise is six feet long and the average among the seal species little less. Killers hunt in packs, and not even the great whales themselves are safe from them; the pack goes for the mighty tongue which in itself may weigh a ton, and when it is torn out the giant bleeds to death while the Killers feed.

As I write there lies a few hundred yards down the shore the newly-dead body of a brown seal. The forepart of the head has gone, where something has crunched through the skull in front of the eyes, and from one flank there has been ripped away a foot length of flesh and blubber, exposing the entrails. There are other possible solutions, though none of them likely; it is the typical work of a Killer in killing mood. On Hyskeir the lighthouse men have told me how they have seen the Killers slash seals for sport and not for food, and leave them maimed and dying among the skerries.

A Killer or two comes every year to Camusfeàrna, but they do not linger, and if they did I would compass their deaths by any means that I could, for they banish the other sea life from my surroundings; also, I do not care to be among them in a small boat. There are many tales, but few, if any, authenticated records, of their attacking human beings; however, I do not want to be the first. Last year a single bull terrorized the tiny harbour of the Isle of Canna the summer through; John Lorne-Campbell shared my aversion to being a guinea-pig for dietary research among Killers, and wrote asking my advice about its destruction. I smugly advised him to shoot it, and gave reasoned instructions as to the precise moment and bull's eye, but I was thirty miles away, and I daresay my advice did not seem as sound and constructive on Canna as it did to me at Camusfeàrna.

No strange sea monster has ever come my way since I have been here, though in the summer of 1959 there was something not easily explicable close by. It was seen by Tex Geddes, once a harpoon gunner in the Island of Soay Shark Fisheries, and now the owner of the island, and by an English visitor whom he had taken out fishing in his boat.

On Sunday 13th September, he took this visitor, a Mr. Gavin, an engineer from Hertfordshire, to fish for mackerel off the southern tip of Soay. It was a hot, flat-calm day, with every object at the sea's surface visible for miles. At about four o'clock in the afternoon Mr. Gavin drew Tex's attention to a large black object about a mile away in the direction of Loch Slapin. The mackerel were playing on the surface and making the sea boil all round the boat, so Tex did not at first take any notice, and went on fishing, facing in the opposite direction. The object, however, drew steadily nearer, and at length both men stopped fishing in order to watch it. When it was some two hundred yards away Tex noticed a party of five Killer whales not far off in the direction of the Island of Rhum. Tex trusts Killers no more than I do; in the words of his letter to me the next day: 'I was not sure what kind of a thing this was that was slowly making up on us—it certainly did not look like a Killer, but nevertheless I was not over thrilled.'

As it drew near, he first thought that it was a tortoise or a turtle, but as it came abreast of the boat he changed his mind. The head of the creature was about two-and-a-half feet out of the water, a head that had 'two huge round eyes like apples', and what Mr. Gavin described as the head of a tortoise magnified to the size of a donkey's. There was a gash-like mouth, with pronounced lips, occupying about half of the head's circumference. The mouth opened and shut rhythmically, showing a red interior and emitting a wheezing sound that reminded Tex of a cow with pleurisy. He could see neither nostrils nor ears. Some two feet behind the head the back showed, higher than the head, and eight feet or more long; it rose steeply to a gradual fall aft, dark brown, but not as dark as the head. This back was not smooth but 'rose out of the water like the Cuillin hills', as Tex wrote in his letter to me the next day. The impression, he said, was of an animal weighing some five tons.

At its nearest point the creature was no more than fifteen or twenty yards from Tex's boat; it passed travelling at five knots or so, heading SSW towards Barra.

Every detail of this story is corroborated by Tex's companion, and in such ideal conditions of visibility and proximity it would be difficult for either or both men to have been victims of optical illusion. It is not, incidentally, the first tale, or even the second, of monsters in the vicinity of Soay.

My old quarry the Basking Sharks I have seen but seldom since they ceased to be my bread and butter, or rather my quest for bread and butter. The first Basking Shark with which I ever came to grips, sixteen crowded years ago was, by a strange coincidence, just out to sea from Camusfeàrna lighthouse, but in the ten years on and off that I have lived here since, I have only seen sharks on a bare half-dozen occasions, and most of them a long way off. No doubt they have often been showing at times when I was not there to see them. Only once have I seen them right close inshore, and then they were being hunted by my successors: I had been sitting up all night with my dog Jonnie, who was at the very edge of death and I was too crushed with sadness and weariness to identify myself with that strange vignette of my past life.

The stages of Jonnie's illness have become blurred in my mind; the two crises from which he made miraculous but ephemeral recoveries seem no longer related in sequence. I had been in London, and travelled to Camusfeàrna in the last week of April. Morag had telephoned to me to tell me that Jonnie was not well, and by the time I arrived he had developed pneumonia; he was a dog of enormous strength, but he was growing old, and his heart was not a young dog's heart.

At the end of one despairing night sitting with him at Druimfiaclach, Morag relieved me after she had seen to her family's
wants, and I set off down the hill for Camusfeàrna, dazed and
unhappy and longing desperately to get into bed and sleep. When
I came to the part of the track that looks down over the house and
the sea I was startled by the unmistakable boom of a harpoon gun,
and woke, as it were, to find myself staring straight into the past.
Below me in the calm bay was a ringnet boat from Mallaig; there
was a storm of thrashing spray about her bows, and from the gun
in her stem drifted a thin haze of cordite smoke. A little farther
out to sea were showing the vast dorsal fins of two more sharks.
I saw the white water at the boat's bows subside as the harpooned
shark sounded, and I sat and watched the whole familiar procedure as they got the winches started and hauled for half an hour
before they had him back at the surface; I saw that great six-foot
tail break water and lash and slam the boat's sides while they
struggled, as I had struggled so often before, to lasso the wildly
lunging target; I saw it captured and made fast—yet because of
my own state of exhaustion and preoccupation the whole scene
was utterly without meaning to me, and I had no moment of
mental participation while the small figures of the crew scurried
about the deck in pursuance of a routine that had once been my
daily life. Yet at other times, when I have watched through the
field glasses the cruising fins of sharks far down the Sound, I have
been possessed by a wild and entirely illogical unrest; the same
sort of unrest, I imagine, that migratory creatures feel in captivity
when the season for their movement is at hand.

Though Jonnie survived pneumonia to become seemingly as strong as before, the writing was on the wall. A few months later he developed cancer of the rectum, and while it was, I think, painless, he had always been a dog of great dignity and cleanliness, and he felt acutely the concomitant humiliation of an evil-smelling discharge over the white silk-and-wool of his coat. When I was away from Camusfeàrna he lived with Morag MacKinnon, to whom he accorded a devotion no less than to myself, but when I came back after months of absence he would go mad with joy like a puppy and lead the way down the path to Camusfeàrna as if I had never left it. But it was with Morag that he died at last, for I was too cowardly to travel north and watch my old friend killed, as in all humanity he had to be.

Camusfeàrna is a very long way from a vet.; the nearest, in fact, is on the Island of Skye, nearly fifty miles away by road and ferry-boat. When he visited Jonnie that winter of 1954 he said that the disease was progressing very rapidly, and that pain when it came would be sudden and acute, with a complete blockage of the rectum. He thought there was a fifty-fifty chance of Jonnie surviving what would now be a major operation, but he was insistent that action must be taken at once either to end Jonnie's life or to prolong it.

I had no car with me that year, so I hired one for the whole journey, to wait during the operation and to bring me back at night, either alone or with what I was warned would in any event be an unconscious dog. Jonnie loved car journeys, and he was enthusiastic to start on this one; as we bumped over the precipitous road to the ferry he stuck his head out of the window and quested the breeze with all the zest of his puppyhood long ago, and I was miserable to see in some sense his trust betrayed and to know that in the evening I might come back alone and leave him dead in Skye. All I could think of then and during the long long wait while he was on the operating table was of past days spent with Jonnie, many of them seeming so long ago as to span a man's rather than a dog's lifetime. I stayed to help to give the anaesthetic; Jonnie was trusting but puzzled by the curious preparations, hating the stinking rubber mask that I had to hold over his face, but giving only one pathetic whimper of despair before he lost consciousness. Then for more than an hour I wandered aimlessly up and down the shore below that Skye village. The day was grey and heavy with coming snow, and a bitter little wind blew in from the sea and rustled the dead seaweed on the tideline. I thought of how I had nursed Jonnie through distemper twelve years before; of teaching that strangely woolly spaniel puppy to retrieve and to quarter the ground for game; of how once in his early prime he had, after an evening duck flight, swum out forty-one times through forming ice that skinned over behind him as he swam and returned forty-one times with a wigeon in his mouth; of how often his fleecy flank had formed a pillow for me in open boats; of the many times I had come back to Camusfeàrna knowing that his welcome was awaiting me.

I have more than once tried to analyse this apparently deliberate form of self-torture that seems common to so many people in face of the extinction of a valued life, human or animal, and it springs, I think, from a negation of death, as if by summoning and arranging these subjective images one were in some way cheating the objective fact. It is, I believe, an entirely instinctive process, and the distress it brings with it is an incidental, a by-product, rather than a masochistic end.

But Jonnie did not die then. When I was allowed to go into the surgery he was conscious but too weak to move; only his blood-stained tail fluttered faintly, and all through the cruelly long and jolting journey home he lay utterly motionless, so that again and again I felt for his heart to make sure that he was still living. It was night before we reached Druimfiaclach, and the snow had begun, piling in thick before an icy north wind. Morag, whose whole heart had gone out to Jonnie from the first day he had come to Druimfiaclach, had endured a longer suspense than I, but though Jonnie was living he yet seemed very near to death. For many days there was little change; either Morag or I would sit up with him all through the night and tend his helplessness. His very cleanliness provided the worst problem of all; while he was too weak to move he would yet endure agonies rather than relieve himself indoors, so that he had to be carried outside in that bitter weather and supported to keep him upright while one or other of us screened him with a blanket from the wind and the snow.

Jonnie recovered from the operation as only a dog of his tremendous physique could do, and for six months his prime was miraculously restored, but in the autumn the cancer came back, and this time it was inoperable. Morag wrote to tell me of this, and to ask my assent to his death before the pain should start and while he was as yet happy and active. I agreed with a heavy heart, not least because I knew that to make the arrangements for his death while he felt himself sound in wind and limb would be a torture to Morag; but, weighed down at the time by a bitter human loss, I lacked the courage to go north and take an active hand in things myself. Jonnie received the vet. with enthusiasm, and Morag cuddled Jonnie while he received a lethal injection. He gave no sign of feeling the needle, and she only knew that he was dead by the increasing heaviness of his head in her hand. Morag had given her heart to Jonnie as she had to no other animal in her life, and for her that moment of betrayal must have been like death itself.

I have never had another dog since Jonnie; I have not wanted one, and shall not, perhaps, until I am of an age that would not be congenial to an active dog.

6

WHILE I was quite clear that I did not want to own another dog, and that Jonnie's death had in some sense ended an overlong chapter of nostalgia in my life, it was, I think, autumn and winter's days at Camusfeàrna that with their long hours of darkness made me crave for some animal life about the house.

Autumn begins for me with the first day on which the stags roar. Because the wind is nearly always in the west, and because the fences keep the bulk of the stags to the higher ground above Camusfeàrna, behind the low mass of the littoral hills, I hear them first on the steep slopes of Skye across the Sound, a wild, haunting primordial sound that belongs so utterly to the north that I find it difficult to realize that stags must roar, too, in European woodlands where forests are composed of trees instead of windswept mountain slopes. It is the first of the cold weather that leads in the rut, and the milder the season the later the stags break out, but it is usually during the last ten days of September. Often the first of the approaching fall comes with a night frost and clear, sharp, blue days, with the bracken turning red, the rowan berries already scarlet, and the ground hardening underfoot; so garish are the berries and the turning leaves in sunshine that in Glengarry a post-office-red pillar-box standing alone by the roadside merges, for a few weeks, anonymously into its background.

When the full moon comes at this season I have sat on the hillside at night and listened to the stags answering one another from hill to hill all round the horizon, a horizon of steel-grey peaks among moving silver clouds and the sea gleaming white at their feet, and high under the stars the drifting chorus of the wild geese flying southward out of the night and north.

On such a night, before I ever came to Camusfeàrna, I slept

70

beside a lochan on the Island of Soay, and it was the wild swans that called overhead and came spiralling down, ghostly in the moonlight, to alight with a long rush of planing feet on the lochan's surface. All through the night I heard their restless murmur as they floated light as spume upon the peat-dark waves, and their soft voices became blended with my dreams, so that the cool convex of their breasts became my pillow. At dawn their calling awoke me as they gathered to take flight, and as they flew southward I watched the white pulse of their wings until I could see them no longer. To me they were a symbol, for I was saying good-bye to Soay, that had been my island.

Winters at Camusfeàrna vary as they do elsewhere, but at their worst they are very bad indeed. When one gets up in darkness to the lashing of rain on the window-panes and the roar of the waterfall rising even above the howl of wind and tide; when the green field is scattered with wide pools that are in part floodwater but in part the overspill of waves whose spray batters the house itself; when day by day the brief hours of light are filled with dark scudding clouds and blown spindrift from the crashing shore, one begins to know the meaning of an isolation that in summer seemed no more than an empty word.

The burn fills and runs ramping high through the trunks and limbs of the alders, carrying racing masses of débris that lodge among their branches, and through the roaring of its passage comes the hollow undertone of rolling, bumping boulders swept along its bed by the weight of white water pouring from the rock ravine. It was in such a spate as this that the bridge was washed away in 1953, and then for five years the only alternative, when the burn was full, to braving that crazy crossing clinging to a stretched rope was the long route to Druimfiaclach by the near side of its course, more than two miles of steep ground and sodden peat bog. Since the gales tear in from the south-west, funnelling themselves between the Hebridean islands into demoniac fury, the wind is usually at one's back on the upward journey, but it is in one's face coming down, and there have been nights returning from Druimfiaclach, torchless and in utter darkness, when I have taken to my hands and knees to avoid being swept away like a leaf.

There is, of course, another side to the picture, the bright log fire whose flames are reflected on the pine-panelled walls, the warmth and nursery security of that kitchen sitting-room with the steady reassuring hiss of its Tilley lamps as a foreground sound to the tumult of sea and sky without; and, in the old days, Jonnie asleep conventionally on the hearth rug. But Jonnie was gone, and all too often the other pigments, as it were, for this picture were lacking too. The supply of paraffin would run out during the short dark days; candles became unobtainable within a hundred road miles; there was not space to store enough dry wood to keep the house heated. Until this year, when I installed a Calor gas stove, I cooked entirely by Primus, requiring both methylated spirits and paraffin, and when the house was without either and it would require an hour to coax a kettle to the boil over a fire of wet wood, there have been days when a kind of apathy would settle down upon me, days when I would rather creep back to bed than face the physical difficulties of life awake. When stores do arrive they have still to be lugged down the hill from Druimfiaclach, a long stumbling journey with an un-balancing load upon one's back and sleet slashing at one's face and eyes; and above all I remember in the past the chill, inhospitable familiarity of wet clothes, wet clothes hanging in rows above a barely-smouldering fire and with as much hope of drying as the sea itself.

Sometimes there is snow, though it rarely lies deep at Camus-feàrna itself, as the house can be no more than six feet above sea-

72

level. But I remember one winter when it did, and it lay thick round the house and came swirling in gustily from the sea on the morning that I had to depart for the south. I left the house before dawn to catch the mail Land Rover at Druimfiaclach, the darkness only just relieved by the white wastes that ran right down to the waves. I remember that morning particularly because it was the worst, the most nightmarish, climb that I have ever made to Druimfiaclach. The weather had been so bitter that the burn was low, frozen far up its course on the snow peak, and I had thought that with the aid of the rope I should be able to ford it in long seamen's thigh-boots. I saw my mistake when I reached it, but with a hundredweight or so of luggage on my back I preferred to try rather than to take the long route round through the bogs. Both my boots filled in the first couple of yards, but the house was locked and time was short, and I struggled across, soaked at last to the waist, hanging on to the rope with my legs swept downstream by the piling weight of snow water. At the far side of the burn I sat down and emptied my boots of a full two gallons apiece. I tried to wring out my trousers, but when, my teeth chattering like castenets, I got the boots back on again, the feet filled slowly with an icy trickle of water that still coursed down my legs. When I began the steep climb from the burn the burden on my shoulders seemed to have doubled its weight. I slipped and stumbled and panted up dim glaucous slopes that had lost all landmarks, and at the top of the first steep I was caught in a swirling, flurrying blizzard of wind and snowflakes, that spun me round in unsteady pirouettes and left me dizzy and directionless.

For all the hundreds of times that I had travelled this path in daylight and in darkness, I could recognize no curve nor contour in the merging grey pillows about me, and the snow was coming down so thick that it blanketed even the sound of the eighty-foot falls in the gorge. I had always been frightened of a stranger slipping down that precipice in the dark; now I was so hopelessly lost that I began to be afraid of it myself, and to avoid the ravine I began to climb upward over the steepest ground I could find. I reeled into snowdrifts and fell flat on my face, my feet slipped on boulders hidden by the snow and the weight on my shoulders threw me over backwards, and all the time the blizzard beat at me, slapping the wet snow into my eyes and ears, down my neck, and into every crevice of my clothing. Once I stumbled on a stag, snow-blanketed in the shelter of a rock; he was up and away and gone into snowflakes that were driving horizontally across the hill-side, and for some minutes I took his place under the rock, the stag smell pungent in my nostrils, wondering how I had ever thought Camusfeàrna a paradise. It took me an hour and a half to reach Druimfiaclach that morning, and when I got there it was more by accident than judgment. This was the prelude to an hour's travel by launch and four hours in the train to Inverness before starting the true journey south.

Yet it is the best and the worst that one remembers, seldom the mediocrities that lie between and demand no attention. At the end of struggles such as those there has always been the warmth and hospitality of the long-suffering MacKinnon household, Morag's scones and gingerbread, and cups of tea that have tasted like nectar; and there have been fair winter days at Camusfeàrna, when the sea lay calm as summer and the sun shone on the snow-covered hills of Skye, and I would not change my home for any in the world.

But after Jonnie's death it seemed, as I have said, a little lifeless, and I began in a desultory way to review in my mind various animals, other than dogs, that might keep me company. Having been encouraged in my childhood to keep pets ranging from hedgehogs to herons, I had a considerable list available for screening, but after a while I realized reluctantly that none of these creatures with which I was familiar would meet my present requirements. I put the idea aside, and for a year I thought no more of it.

Early in the New Year of 1956 I travelled with Wilfred Thesiger to spend two months or so among the little known Marsh Arabs, or Ma'dan, of Southern Iraq. By then it had crossed my mind, though with no great emphasis, that I should like to keep an otter instead of a dog, and that Camusfeàrna, ringed by water a stone's throw from its door, would be an eminently suitable spot for this experiment. I had mentioned this casually to

Wilfred soon after the outset of our journey, and he, as casually, had replied that I had better get one in the Tigris marshes before I came home, for there they were as common as mosquitoes, and were often tamed by the Arabs.

We spent the better part of those two months squatting cross-legged in the bottom of a *tarada* or war canoe, travelling in a leisurely, timeless way between the scattered reed-built villages of the great delta marsh both west of the Tigris and between the river and the Persian frontier; and towards the end of our journey I did acquire an otter cub.

It is difficult to find new words in which to tell of happenings that one has already described; if one has done one's best the first time one can only do worse on the second attempt, when the freshness of the image has faded; and that must be my excuse and apology for quoting here part of what I wrote of that otter cub, Chahala, soon afterwards; that and the fact that she is an integral and indispensable part of my narrative.

We were sitting after dark in a *mudhif*, or sheikh's guest house, on a mud island in the marshes, and I was brooding over the delinquency of the chatelaine, a bossy old harridan of a woman who had angered me.

'I felt an unreasonable hatred for that witless woman with her show of bustle and competence, and contempt that not even her avarice had mastered her stupidity. Thinking of these things, I was not trying to understand the conversation around me when the words "celb mai" caught my ear. "What was that about otters?" I asked Thesiger.

' "I think we've got you that otter cub you said you wanted. This fellow comes from that village half a mile away; he says he's had one for about ten days. Very small and sucks milk from a bottle. Do you want it?"

'The otter's owner said he would fetch it and be back in half an hour or so. He got up and went out; through the entrance of the *mudhif* I could see his canoe glide away silently over the star-reflecting water.

'Presently he returned carrying the cub, came across into the firelight and put it down on my knee as I sat cross-legged. It looked up and chittered at me gently. It was the size of a kitten or a squirrel, still a little unsteady on its legs, with a stiff-looking tapering tail the length of a pencil, and it exhaled a wholly delightful malty smell. It rolled over on its back, displaying a round furry stomach and the soles of four webbed feet.

' "Well," said Thesiger, "do you want her?" I nodded. "How much are you prepared to pay for her?"

' "Certainly more than they would ask."

' "I'm not going to pay some ridiculous price—it's bad for prestige. We'll take her if they'll sell her for a reasonable price; if not, we'll get one somewhere else."

'I said, "Let's make certain of getting this one; we're near the end of the time now, and we may not get another chance. And after all the prestige doesn't matter so much, as this is your last visit to the marshes." I saw this fascinating little creature eluding me for the sake of a few shillings' worth of prestige, and the negotiations seemed to me interminable.

'In the end we bought the cub for five dinar, the price to include the rubber teat and the filthy but precious bottle from which she was accustomed to drink. Bottles are a rarity in the marshes.

'Most infant animals are engaging, but this cub had more charm per cubic inch of her tiny body than all the young animals I had ever seen. Even now I cannot write about her without a pang.

'I cut a collar for her from the strap of my field-glasses—a difficult thing, for her head was no wider than her neck—and tied six foot of string to this so as to retain some permanent contact with her if at any time she wandered away from me. Then I slipped her inside my shirt, and she snuggled down at once in a security of warmth and darkness that she had not known since she was reft from her mother. I carried her like that through her short life; when she was awake her head would peer wonderingly out from the top of the pullover, like a kangaroo from its mother's pouch, and when she was asleep she slept as otters like to, on her back with her webbed feet in the air. When she was awake her voice was a bird-like chirp, but in her dreams she would give a wild little cry on three falling notes, poignant and desolate. I called her Chahala, after the river we had left the day before, and because those syllables were the nearest one could write to the sound of her sleeping cry.

'I slept fitfully that night; all the pi-dogs of Dibin seemed to bark at my ears, and I dared not in any case let myself fall into too sound a sleep lest I should crush Chahala, who now snuggled in my armpit. Like all otters, she was "house-trained" from the beginning, and I had made things easy for her by laying my sleeping bag against the wall of the *mudhif*, so that she could step straight out on the patch of bare earth between the reed columns. This she did at intervals during the night, backing into the very farthest corner to produce, with an expression of infinite concentration, a tiny yellow caterpillar of excrement. Having inspected this, with evident satisfaction of a job well done, she would clamber up my shoulder and chitter gently for her bottle. This she preferred to drink lying on her back and holding the bottle between her paws as do bear cubs, and when she had finished sucking she would fall sound asleep with the teat still in her mouth and a beatific expression on her baby face.

'She accepted me as her parent from the moment that she first fell asleep in my pullover, and never once did she show fear of anything or anyone, but it was as a parent that I failed her, for I had neither the knowledge nor the instinct of her mother, and when she died it was because of my ignorance. Meanwhile this tragedy, so small but so complete, threw no shadow on her brief life, and as the days went by she learned to know her name and to play a little as a kitten does, and to come scuttling along at my heels if I could find dry land to walk on, for she hated to get her feet wet. When she had had enough of walking she would chirp and paw at my legs until I squatted down so that she could dive head first into the friendly darkness inside my pullover; sometimes she would at once fall asleep in that position, head downward with the tip of her pointed tail sticking out at the top. The Arabs called her my daughter, and used to ask me when I had last given her suck.

'I soon found that she was restrictive of movement and activity. Carried habitually inside my pullover, she made an enceinte-looking bulge which collected a whole village round me as soon as I set foot outside the door; furthermore I could no longer carry my camera round my neck as I did normally, for it bumped against her body as I walked.

'One evening Thesiger and I discussed the prospect of weaning Chahala. We both felt she she should be old enough to eat solid food, and I felt that her rather skinny little body would benefit by something stronger than buffalo milk. However, I under-estimated the power of instinct, for I thought that she would not connect flesh or blood with edibility and would need to be introduced to the idea very gradually. The best way to do this, I decided, was to introduce a few droops of blood into her milk to get her used to the taste. This proved to be extraordinarily naïve, for while I was holding the bodies of two decapitated sparrows and trying to drip a little blood from them into her feeding bottle she suddenly caught the scent of the red meat and made a savage grab for the carcasses. I think that if I had not stopped her she would have crunched up bone and all with those tiny needle-like teeth, and we took this as evidence that she had already been introduced by her mother to adult food. I took the carcasses from her, much to her evident fury; and when I gave her the flesh from the breasts cut up small she wolfed it down savagely and went questing round for more.

' "Finish with milk," said Amara, our chief canoe-boy, with a gesture of finality, "finish, finish; she is grown up now." And it seemed so, but, alas, she was not.

'A week later we shot a Buff-backed Heron for her, and she wolfed the shredded flesh avidly. It was the last food that she ate.

'It was very cold that night. Over my head was a gap in the reed matting of the roof through which the stars showed bright and unobscured, but a thin wind that seemed as chill as the tinkle of icicles rustled the dry reeds at the foot of the wall, and I slept fitfully. Chahala was restless and would not stay still in my sleeping bag; I did not know that she was dying, and I was impatient with her. In the morning I took her to a spit of dry land beyond the edge of the village to let her walk, and only then I realized that she was very ill. She would not move, but lay

78

looking up at me pathetically, and when I picked her up again she instantly sought the warm darkness inside my pullover.

'We made an hour's journey through flower-choked waterways in low green marsh, and stopped at another big island village. It was plain to me when we landed that Chahala was dying. She was weak but restless, and inside the house she sought the dark corners between the reed columns and the matting walls. She lay belly downward, breathing fast and in obvious distress. Perhaps something in our huge medicine chest could have saved her, but we thought only of castor oil, for everything she had eaten the night before was still inside her. The oil had little effect, and though she sucked almost automatically from her bottle there was little life in her. I sat hopelessly beside her for a couple of hours when Thesiger came in from doctoring. "Better get out for a bit," he said. "I'll keep an eye on her. It's hell for you sitting in here all the time, and you can't do her any good. This is your last marsh village, and you may never see another."

'I went out, and remembered things that I had wanted to photograph and always postponed. Then I found that the shutter of my camera was broken, and I went back into the house.

'We left an hour later. When I felt the warmth of Chahala next to my shirt again I felt a moment's spurious comfort that she would live; but she would not stay there. She climbed out with a strength that surprised me, and stretched herself restlessly on the floor of the canoe, and I spread a handkerchief over my knees to make an awning of shade for her small fevered body. Once she called faintly, the little wild lonely cry that would come from her as she slept, and a few seconds after that I saw a shiver run through her body. I put my hand on her and felt the strange rigidity that comes in the instant following death; then she became limp under my touch.

' "She's dead," I said. I said it in Arabic, so that the boys would stop paddling.

'Thesiger said, "Are you sure?" and the boys stared unbelievingly. "Quite dead?" they asked it again and again. I handed her to Thesiger; the body drooped from his hands like a miniature fur stole. "Yes," he said, "she's dead." He threw the body into the water, and it landed in the brilliant carpet of white and golden flowers and floated on its back with the webbed paws at its sides, as she had been used to sleep when she was alive.

' "Come on," said Thesiger. "Ru-hu-Ru-hu!" but the boys sat motionless, staring at the small corpse and at me, and Thesiger grew angry with them before they would move. Amara kept on looking back from the bows until at last we rounded the corner of a green reed-bed and she was out of sight.

'The sun shone on the white flowers, the blue kingfishers glinted low over them and the eagles wheeled overhead on the blue sky, but all of these seemed less living for me since Chahala was dead. I told myself that she was only one of thousands like her in these marshes, that are speared with the five-pointed trident, or shot, or taken as cubs to die slowly in more callous captivity, but she was dead and I was desolate. The fault lay with whoever, perhaps more than a million years ago, had first taken up the wild dog cub that clung to the body of its dead dam, and I wondered whether he too had in that half-animal brain been driven by the motives that in me were conscious.'

I fretted miserably over the death of Chahala, for she had convinced me utterly that it was an otter that I wanted as an animal companion at Camusfeàrna, and I felt that I had had my chance and wasted it. It was not until long afterwards that the probable cause of her death struck me. The Marsh Arabs drug fish with digitalis concealed in shrimp bait, and whereas the human system, or that of an adult Buff-backed Heron, might find the minute dose innocuous, the same quantity might be fatal to as young a creature as Chahala.

I had no more time in the marshes; Wilfred and I were to spend a few days in Basra before going on to pass the early summer among the pastoral tribes. But Chahala's death, which seemed to me like an end, was in fact a beginning.

PART II

Living with Otters

7

THE NIGHT that Chahala died we reached Al Azair, Ezra's tomb, on the Tigris. From there Wilfred Thesiger and I were both going to Basra to collect and answer our mail from Europe before setting off together again. At the Consulate-General at Basra we found that Wilfred's mail had arrived but that mine had not.

'I cabled to England, and when, three days later, nothing had happened, I tried to telephone. The call had to be booked twenty-four hours in advance, and could be arranged only for a single hour in the day, an hour during which, owing to the difference in time, no one in London was likely to be available. On the first day the line was out of order; on the second the exchange was closed for a religious holiday. On the third day there was another break-down. I arranged to join Thesiger at Abd el Nebi's *mudhif* in a week's time, and he left.

'Two days before the date of our rendezvous I returned to the Consulate-General late in the afternoon, after several hours' absence, to find that my mail had arrived. I carried it to my bedroom to read, and there squatting on the floor were two Marsh Arabs; beside them lay a sack that squirmed from time to time.

'They handed me a note from Thesiger. "Here is your otter, a male and weaned. I feel you may want to take it to London—it would be a handful in the *tarada*. It is the one I originally heard of, but the sheikhs were after it, so they said it was dead. Give Ajram a letter to me saying it has arrived safely—he has taken Kathia's place. . . ." '

With the opening of that sack began a phase of my life that in the essential sense has not yet ended, and may, for all I know, not end before I do. It is, in effect, a thraldom to otters, an otter fixation, that I have since found to be shared by most other people who have ever owned one.

The creature that emerged, not greatly disconcerted, from this sack on to the spacious tiled floor of the Consulate bedroom did not at that moment resemble anything so much as a very small medievally-conceived dragon. From the head to the tip of the tail he was coated with symmetrical pointed scales of mud armour, between whose tips was visible a soft velvet fur like that of a chocolate-brown mole. He shook himself, and I half expected this aggressive camouflage to disintegrate into a cloud of dust, but it remained unaffected by his manoeuvre, and in fact it was not for another month that I contrived to remove the last of it and see him, as it were, in his true colours.

Yet even on that first day I recognized that he was an otter of a species that I had never seen in the flesh, resembling only a curious otter skin that I had bought from the Arabs in one of the marsh villages. Mijbil, as I called the new otter, after a sheikh with whom we had recently been staying and whose name had intrigued me with a conjured picture of a platypus-like creature, was, in fact, of a race previously unknown to science, and was at length christened by zoologists, from examination of the skin and of himself, *Lutrogale perspicillata maxwelli*, or Maxwell's otter. This circumstance, perhaps, influenced on my side the intensity of the emotional relationship between us, for I became, during a year of his constant and violently affectionate companionship, fonder of him than of almost any human being, and to write of him in the past tense makes me feel as desolate as one who has lost an only child. For a year and five days he was about my bed and my bath spying out all my ways, and though I now have another otter no whit less friendly and fascinating, there will never be another Mijbil.

For the first twenty-four hours Mijbil was neither hostile nor friendly; he was simply aloof and indifferent, choosing to sleep on the floor as far from my bed as possible, and to accept food and water as though they were things that had appeared before him without human assistance. The food presented a problem, for it did not immediately occur to me that the Marsh Arabs had almost certainly fed him on rice scraps only supplemented by such portions of fish as are inedible to humans. The Consul-General sent out a servant to buy fish, but this servant's return coincided with a visit from Robert Angorly, a British-educated Christian Iraqi who was the Crown Prince's game warden and entertained a passionate interest in natural history. Angorly told me that none of the fishes that had been bought was safe for an animal, for they had been poisoned with digitalis, which, though harmless to a human in this quantity, he felt certain would be dangerous to a young otter. He offered to obtain me a daily supply of fish that had been taken with nets, and thereafter he brought every day half a dozen or so small reddish fish from the Tigris. These Mijbil consumed with gusto, holding them upright between his forepaws, tail end uppermost, and eating them like a stick of Edinburgh rock, always with five crunches of the left-hand side of the jaw alternating with five crunches on the right.

It was fortunate that I had recently met Angorly, for otherwise Mijbil might at once have gone the way of Chahala and for the same reason. Angorly had called at the Consulate-General during the time that I had been waiting for my mail from Europe, and had invited me to a day's duck shooting on the Crown Prince's fabulous marshes, an experience that nobody can ever have again, for now the hated Crown Prince is as dead as only a mob gone berserk could make him, and of my friend Angorly, whom I cannot believe ever to have taken much interest in anything political, there has been no word since the revolution.

Of the duck shoot my most enduring memory is of a great cloud of pink flamingos flying at head height to my butt, and of the rank upon rank of crimson and white wings rustling low over my head. Duck there were in thousands, but if the Crown Prince ever killed many from that butt he was a better man than I. It stood quite alone in a great waste of unbroken water that stretched away for a mile or more in all directions; its sides were no more than waist high, and in the centre of it was a wooden seat, at the right of which pretention stood an object like a bird-table, whose tray was designed to hold eight unopened boxes of twenty-five cartridges. It held them, and the broad scarlet patch that they formed flared a warning to every duck that came within two hundred yards. I was the cynosure of every bird's eye in the place. The floor of the butt was six inches under water, so the cartridges remained where they were, and the duck did not. After some five hours I was rescued from my indignity, and Angorly and I between us took home some hundred and fifty duck, of which I had contributed a meagre third. But the flamingoes were magnificent.

The otter and I enjoyed the Consul-General's long-suffering hospitality for a fortnight. The second night Mijbil came on to my bed in the small hours and remained asleep in the crook of my knees until the servant brought tea in the morning, and during that day he began to lose his apathy and take a keen, much too keen, interest in his surroundings. I fashioned a collar, or rather a body-belt, for him, and took him on a lead to the bathroom, where for half an hour he went wild with joy in the water, plunging and rolling in it, shooting up and down the length of the bath underwater, and making enough slosh and splash for a hippo. This, I was to learn, is a characteristic of otters; every drop of water must be, so to speak, extended and spread about the place; a bowl must at once be overturned, or, if it will not overturn, be sat in and sploshed in until it overflows. Water must be kept on the move and made to do things; when static it is as wasted and provoking as a buried talent.

It was only two days later that he escaped from my bedroom as I entered it, and I turned to see his tail disappearing round the bend of the corridor that led to the bathroom. By the time I had caught up with him he was up on the end of the bath and fumbling at the chromium taps with his paws. I watched, amazed by this early exhibition of an intelligence I had not yet guessed; in less than a minute he had turned the tap far enough to produce a dribble of water, and, after a moment or two of distraction at his success, achieved the full flow. (He had, in fact, been fortunate to turn the tap the right way; on subsequent occasions he would as often as not try with great violence to screw it up still tighter, chittering with irritation and disappointment at its failure to co-operate.)

The Consulate had a big walled garden in which I exercised him, and, within it, a high-netted tennis court. In this enclosure I established after a few days that he would follow me without a lead and come to me when I called his name. By the end of a week he had accepted me in a relationship of dependence, and with this security established he began to display the principal otter characteristic of perpetual play. Very few species of animal habitually play after they are adult; they are concerned with eating, sleeping, or procreating, or with the means to one or other of these ends. But otters are one of the few exceptions to this rule; right through their lives they spend much of their time in play that does not even require a partner. In the wild state they will play alone for hours with any convenient floating object in the water, pulling it down to let it bob up again, or throwing it with a jerk of the head so that it lands with a splash and becomes a quarry to be pursued. No doubt in their holts they lie on their backs and play, too, as my otters have, with small objects that they can roll between their paws and pass from palm to palm, for at Camusfeàrna all the sea holts contain a profusion of small shells and round stones that can only have been carried in for toys.

Mij would spend hours shuffling a rubber ball round the room like a four-footed soccer player using all four feet to dribble the ball, and he could also throw it, with a powerful flick of the neck, to a surprising height and distance. These games he would play either by himself or with me, but the really steady play of an otter, the time-filling play born of a sense of well-being and a full stomach, seems to me to be when the otter lies on its back and juggles with small objects between its paws. This they do with an extraordinarily concentrated absorption and dexterity, as though a conjuror were trying to perfect some trick, as though in this play there were some goal that the human observer could not guess. Later, marbles became Mij's favourite toys for this pastime —for pastime it is, without any anthropomorphizing—and he would lie on his back rolling two or more of them up and down his wide, flat belly without ever dropping one to the floor, or, with forepaws upstretched, rolling them between his palms for minutes on end.

Even during that first fortnight in Basra I learnt a lot of Mij's language, a language largely shared, I have discovered, by many other races of otter, though with curious variations in usage. The sounds are widely different in range. The simplest is the call note, which has been much the same in all the otters I have come across; it is a short, anxious, penetrating, though not loud, mixture between a whistle and a chirp. There is also a query, used at closer quarters; Mij would enter a room, for instance, and ask whether there was anyone in it by the word 'Ha!", uttered in a loud, harsh whisper. If he saw preparations being made to take him out or to the bath, he would stand at the door making a musical bubbling sound interspersed with chirps; but it was the chirp, in all its permutations and combinations of high and low, from the single querulous note to a continuous flow of chitter, that was Mij's main means of vocal communication. He had one other note unlike any of these, a high, snarling caterwaul, a sort of screaming wail, that meant unequivocally that he was very angry, and if provoked further would bite. He bit, in anger as opposed to nips in excitable play, four times during the year that I had him. Each of these occasions was memorable in the highest degree, though I was only once at the receiving end.

An otter's jaws are, of course, enormously powerful—indeed the whole animal is of strength almost unbelievable in a creature of its size—and those jaws are equipped with teeth to crunch into instant pulp fish heads that seem as hard as stone. Like a puppy that nibbles and gnaws one's hands because he has so few other outlets for his feelings, otters seem to find the use of their mouths the most natural outlet for expression; knowing as I do their enormous crushing power I can appreciate what efforts my otters have made to be gentle in play, but their playful nips are gauged, perhaps, to the sensitivity of an otter's, rather than a human, skin. Mij used to look hurt and surprised when scolded for what must have seemed to him the most meticulous gentleness, and though after a time he learned to be as soft mouthed as a sucking dove with me he remained all his life somewhat over-excitably good-humoured and hail-fellow-well-bit with strangers.

The days passed peacefully at Basra, but I dreaded dismally the

87

unpostponable prospect of transporting Mij to England, and to his ultimate destination, Camusfeàrna. B.O.A.C. would not fly livestock at all, and there was then no other line to London. Finally I booked a Trans-World flight to Paris, with a doubtful Air France booking on the same evening to London. Trans-World insisted that Mij should be packed into a box of not more than eighteen inches square, and that this box must be personal luggage, to be carried on the floor at my feet.

Mij's body was at that time perhaps a little over a foot long and his tail another foot; the designing of this box employed many anxious hours for myself and the ever-helpful Robert Angorly, and finally he had the container constructed by craftsmen of his acquaintance. The box was delivered on the afternoon before my departure on a 9.15 p.m. flight. It was zinc-lined, and divided into two compartments, one for sleeping and one for the relief of nature, and it appeared to my inexperienced eye as nearly ideal as could be contrived.

Dinner was at eight, and I thought that it would be as well to put Mij into the box an hour before we left, so that he would become accustomed to it before the jolting of the journey began to upset him. I manoeuvred him into it, not without difficulty, and he seemed peaceful when I left him in the dark for a hurried meal.

But when I returned, with only barely time for the Consulate car to reach the airport for the flight, I was confronted with an appalling spectacle. There was complete silence from inside the box, but from its airholes and the chinks around the hinged lid, blood had trickled and dried on the white wood. I whipped off the padlock and tore open the lid, and Mij, exhausted and blood-spattered, whimpered and tried to climb up my leg. He had torn the zinc lining to shreds, scratching his mouth, his nose and his paws, and had left it jutting in spiky ribbons all around the walls and the floor of the box. When I had removed the last of it, so that there were no cutting edges left, it was just ten minutes until the time of the flight, and the airport was five miles distant. It was hard to bring myself to put the miserable Mij back into that box, that now represented to him a torture chamber, but I forced myself to do it, slamming the lid down on my fingers as I closed it before he could make his escape. Then began a journey the like of which I hope I shall never know again.

I sat in the back of the car with the box beside me as the Arab driver tore through the streets of Basra like a ricochetting bullet. Donkeys reared, bicycles swerved wildly, out in the suburbs goats stampeded and poultry found unguessed powers of flight. Mij cried unceasingly in the box, and both of us were hurled to and fro and up and down like drinks in a cocktail shaker. Exactly as we drew to a screeching stop before the airport entrance I heard a splintering sound from the box beside me, and saw Mij's nose force up the lid. He had summoned all the strength in his small body and torn one of the hinges clean out of the wood.

The aircraft was waiting to take off; as I was rushed through the customs by infuriated officials I was trying all the time to hold down the lid of the box with one hand, and with the other, using a screwdriver purloined from the driver, to force back the screws into the splintered wood. But I knew that it could be no more than a temporary measure at best, and my imagination boggled at the thought of the next twenty-four hours.

It was perhaps my only stroke of fortune that the seat booked for me was at the extreme front of the aircraft, so that I had a bulkhead before me instead of another seat. The other passengers, a remarkable cross-section of the orient and occident, stared curiously as the dishevelled late arrival struggled up the gangway with a horrifyingly vocal Charles Addams-like box, and knowing for just what a short time it could remain closed I was on tenterhooks to see what manner of passenger would be my immediate neighbour. I had a moment of real dismay when I saw her to be an elegantly dressed and *soignée* American woman in early middle age. Such a one, I thought, would have little sympathy or tolerance for the draggled and dirty otter cub that would so soon and so inevitably be in her midst. For the moment the lid held, and as I sat down and fastened my safety belt there seemed to be a temporary silence from within.

The port engines roared, and then the starboard and the aircraft

89

trembled and teetered against the tug of her propellers, and then we were taxiing out to take off, and I reflected that whatever was to happen now there could be no escape from it, for the next stop was Cairo. Ten minutes later we were flying westwards over the great marshes that had been Mij's home, and peering downward into the dark I could see the glint of their waters beneath the moon.

I had brought a brief-case full of old newspapers and a parcel of fish, and with these scant resources I prepared myself to withstand a siege. I arranged newspapers to cover all the floor around my feet, rang for the air hostess, and asked her to keep the fish in a cool place. I have retained the most profound admiration for that air hostess, and in subsequent sieges and skirmishes with otters in public places I have found my thoughts turning towards her as a man's mind turns to water in desert wastes. She was the very queen of her kind. I took her into my confidence; the events of the last half hour together with the prospect of the next twenty-four had shaken my equilibrium a little, and I daresay I was not too coherent, but she took it all in her graceful sheer nylon stride, and she received the ill-wrapped fish into her shapely hands as though I were travelling royalty depositing a jewel case with her for safe keeping. Then she turned and spoke with her country-woman on my left. Would I not prefer, she then enquired, to have my pet on my knee? The animal would surely feel happier there, and my neighbour had no objection. I could have kissed her hand in the depth of my gratitude. But, not knowing otters, I was quite unprepared for what followed.

I unlocked the padlock and opened the lid, and Mij was out like a flash. He dodged my fumbling hands with an eel-like wriggle and disappeared at high speed down the fuselage of the aircraft. As I tried to get into the gangway I could follow his progress among the passengers by a wave of disturbance amongst them not unlike that caused by the passage of a stoat through a hen run. There were squawks and shrieks and a flapping of travelling-coats, and half-way down the fuselage a woman stood up on her seat screaming out, 'A rat! A rat!' Then the air hostess reached her, and within a matter of seconds she was seated again and smiling benignly. That goddess, I believe, could have controlled a panic-stricken crowd single-handed.

By now I was in the gangway myself, and, catching sight of Mij's tail disappearing beneath the legs of a portly white-turbaned Indian, I tried a flying tackle, landing flat on my face. I missed Mij's tail, but found myself grasping the sandalled foot of the Indian's female companion; furthermore my face was inexplicably covered in curry. I staggered up babbling inarticulate apology, and the Indian gave me a long silent stare, so utterly expressionless that even in my hypersensitive mood I could deduce from it no meaning whatsoever. I was, however, glad to observe that something, possibly the curry, had won over the bulk of my fellow passengers, and that they were regarding me now as a harmless clown rather than as a dangerous lunatic. The air hostess stepped into the breach once more.

'Perhaps,' she said with the most charming smile, 'it would be better if you resumed your seat, and I will find the animal and bring it to you.' She would probably have said the same had Mij been an escaped rogue elephant. I explained that Mij, being lost and frightened, might bite a stranger, but she did not think so. I returned to my seat.

I heard the ripple of flight and pursuit passing up and down the body of the aircraft behind me, but I could see little. I was craning my neck back over the seat trying to follow the hunt when suddenly I heard from my feet a distressed chitter of recognition and welcome, and Mij bounded on to my knee and began to nuzzle my face and neck. In all the strange world of the aircraft I was the only familiar thing to be found, and in that first spontaneous return was sown the seed of the absolute trust that he accorded me for the rest of his life.

For the next hour or two he slept in my lap, descending from time to time for copious evacuations upon the newspaper at my feet, and each time I had, with an unrehearsed legerdemain, to spirit this out of sight and replace it with fresh newspaper. Whenever he appeared restless I rang for fish and water, for I had a feeling that, like the story-teller of the Arabian Nights, if I failed to keep him entertained retribution would fall upon me.

Otters are extremely bad at doing nothing. That is to say that they cannot, as a dog does, lie still and awake; they are either asleep or entirely absorbed in play or other activity. If there is no acceptable toy, or if they are in a mood of frustration, they will, apparently with the utmost good humour, set about laying the land waste. There is, I am convinced, something positively provoking to an otter about order and tidiness in any form, and the greater the state of confusion that they can create about them the more contented they feel. A room is not properly habitable to them until they have turned everything upside down; cushions must be thrown to the floor from sofas and armchairs, books pulled out of bookcases, wastepaper baskets overturned and the rubbish spread as widely as possible, drawers opened and contents shovelled out and scattered. The appearance of such a room where an otter has been given free rein resembles nothing so much as the aftermath of a burglar's hurried search for some minute and valuable object that he has believed to be hidden. I had never really appreciated the meaning of the word ransacked until I saw what an otter could do in this way.

This aspect of an otter's behaviour is certainly due in part to an intense inquisitiveness that belongs traditionally to a mongoose, but which would put any mongoose to shame. An otter must find out everything and have a hand in everything; but most of all he must know what lies inside any man-made container or beyond any man-made obstruction. This, combined with an uncanny mechanical sense of how to get things open—a sense, indeed of statics and dynamics in general—makes it much safer to remove valuables altogether rather than to challenge the otter's ingenuity by inventive obstructions. But in those days I had all this to learn.

We had been flying for perhaps five hours, and must, I thought, be nearing Cairo, when one of these moods descended upon Mijbil. It opened comparatively innocuously, with an assault upon the newspapers spread carefully round my feet, and in a minute or two the place looked like a street upon which royalty has been given a ticker-tape welcome. Then he turned his attentions to the box, where his sleeping compartment was filled with fine wood-shavings. First he put his head and shoulders in and began to throw these out backwards at enormous speed; then he got in bodily and lay on his back, using all four feet in a pedalling motion to hoist out the remainder. I was doing my best to cope with the litter, but it was like a ship's pumps working against a leak too great for them, and I was hopelessly behind in the race when he turned his attention to my neighbour's canvas Trans-World travel bag on the floor beside him. The zipper gave him pause for no more than seconds; by chance, in all likelihood, he yanked it back and was in head first, throwing out magazines, handkerchiefs, gloves, bottles of pills, tins of ear-plugs and all the personal paraphernalia of long-distance air travel. By the grace of God my neighbour was sleeping profoundly; I managed, un-observed, to haul Mij out by the tail and cram the things back somehow. I hoped that she might leave the aircraft at Cairo, before the outrage was discovered, and to my infinite relief she did so. I was still grappling with Mij when the instruction lights came on as we circled the city, and then we were down on the tarmac with forty minutes to wait.

I think it was at Cairo that I realized what a complex and—to me at that time—unpredictable creature I had acquired. I left the aircraft last, and during all the time that we were grounded he was no more trouble than a well-behaved Pekinese dog. I put the lead on him and exercised him round the edge of the airfield; there were jet aircraft landing and taking off with an appalling din all around us, but he gave no sign of noticing them at all. He trotted along at my side, stopping as a dog does to investigate small smells in the grass, and when I went into the refreshment room for a drink he sat down at my feet as if this were the only life to which he was accustomed.

On our way back to the aircraft an Egyptian official hazarded the first of the many guesses as to his identity that I was to hear during the subsequent months. 'What you got there?' he asked. 'An ermine?'

My troubles really began at Paris, an interminable time later. Mij had slept from time to time, but I had not closed an eye, and it was by now more than thirty-six hours since I had even dozed.

I had to change airports, and, since I knew that Mij could slip his body strap with the least struggle, there was no alternative to putting him back into his box. In its present form, however, the box was useless, for one hinge was dangling unattached from the lid.

Half an hour out from Paris I rang for the last time for fish and water, and explained my predicament to the air hostess. She went forward to the crew's quarters, and returned after a few minutes saying that one of the crew would come and nail down the box and rope it for me. She warned me at the same time that Air France's regulations differed from those of Trans-World, and that from Paris onward the box would have to travel freight and not in the passenger portion of the aircraft.

Mij was sleeping on his back inside my jacket, and I had to steel myself to betray his trust, to force him back into that hateful prison and listen to his pathetic cries as he was nailed up in what had become to me suddenly reminiscent of a coffin. There is a little-understood factor that is responsible for the deaths of many wild animals in shipment; it is generally known as 'travel shock', and the exact causes have yet to be determined. Personally I do not question that it is closely akin to the 'voluntary dying' of which Africans have long been reputed to be capable; life has become no longer tolerable, and the animal *chooses*, quite unconsciously no doubt, to die. It was travel shock that I was afraid might kill Mijbil inside that box, which to him represented a circumstance more terrible than any he had experienced, and I would be unable even to give him the reassuring smell of my hand through the breathing-holes.

We disembarked in torrential rain that formed puddles and lakes all over the tarmac and had reduced my thin, semi-tropical suit to a sodden pulp before even I had entered the bus that was to take me and the three other London-bound passengers across Paris to Orly Airport. I clung to the unwieldy box all this time, in the hope of reducing Mij's unavoidable period of despair after I became separated from it; together with the personal impedimenta that I could not well lose sight of it rendered movement almost impossible, and I felt near to voluntary death myself.

After an hour's wait at Orly, during which Mij's cries had given place to a terrifying silence, I and my three companions were hustled into an aircraft. Mij was wrested from me and disappeared into the darkness on a luggage transporter.

When we arrived at Amsterdam instead of London the company was profusely apologetic. There was no flight to London for a further fifty-five minutes.

I had lost sight of Mij's box altogether and no one seemed to have a very clear idea of what had happened to any of the luggage belonging to the four London-bound passengers. A helpful official suggested that it might still be in Paris, as it must be clearly labelled London and not Amsterdam.

I went to the Air France office and let the tattered shreds of my self-control fly to the winds. In my soaking and dishevelled condition I cannot have cut a very impressive figure, but my anger soared above these handicaps like an eagle on the wind. I said that I was transporting to London a live animal worth many thousands of pounds, that unless it was traced immediately it would die, and I would sue the Company and broadcast their inefficiency throughout the world. The official was under crossfire, for at my elbow an American business man was also threatening legal action. When the shindy was at its height another official arrived and said calmly that our luggage was now aboard a B.E.A. plane due for take-off in seven minutes, and would we kindly take our seats in the bus.

We deflated slowly. Muttering, 'I guess I'm going to cast my personal eyes on that baggage before I get air-borne again. They can't make a displaced person out of me', my American companion spoke for all of us waifs. So we cast our personal eyes into the freight compartment, and there was Mij's box, quite silent in a corner.

It was the small hours of the morning when we reached London Airport. I had cabled London from Amsterdam, and there was a hired car to meet me, but there was one more contretemps before I reached the haven of my flat. In all my travels I have never, but for that once, been required by the British Customs to open a single bag or to do more than state that I carried no goods liable to duty. It was, of course, my fault; the extreme fatigue and nervous tension of the journey had destroyed my diplomacy. I was, for whichever reason, so tired that I could hardly stand, and to the proffered *pro forma* and the question, 'Have you read this?' I replied, with extreme testiness and foolishness, 'Yes—hundreds of times.'

'And you have nothing to declare?'

'Nothing.'

'How long have you been out of this country?'

'About three months.'

'And during that time you have acquired nothing?'

'Nothing but what is on the list I have given you.' (This comprised my few purchases in Iraq; two uncured otter skins, a Marsh Arab's dagger, three cushion covers woven by the Beni Lam tribe, and one live otter.)

He seemed momentarily at a loss, but he had retired only *pour mieux sauter*. The attack, when it came, was utterly unexpected.

'Where did you get that watch?'

I could have kicked myself. Two days before, when playing water games with Mijbil in the bath, I had forgotten to screw in the winding handle of my Rolex Oyster, and it had, not unnaturally, stopped. I had gone into Basra and bought, for twelve shillings and sixpence, an outrageous time-piece that made a noise like castanets. It had stopped twice, unprovoked, during the journey.

I explained, but I had already lost face. I produced my own watch from a pocket, and added that I should be grateful if he would confiscate the replacement forthwith.

'It is not a question of confiscation,' he said, 'there is a fine for failing to declare dutiable goods. And now may I please examine that Rolex?'

It took another quarter of an hour to persuade him that the Rolex was not contraband; then he began to search my luggage. No corner was left unexplored; Mijbil himself could not have done better, and when he had finished none of the cases would close. Then he turned to the last item on my list, one live otter. He pondered this in silence for perhaps a minute. Then, 'You have with you a live otter?' I said that I very much doubted whether it was still alive, but that it had been when at Paris.

'If the animal is dead there will be no duty payable on the un-cured skin; if it is alive it is, of course, subject to the quarantine regulations.'

I had taken the trouble to check this point before leaving Iraq, and at last I was on firm ground. I told him that I knew there to be no quarantine regulations, and that since he had now cleared my luggage I proposed to leave with the otter; if he tried to detain me I would hold him legally responsible for the death of a valuable animal.

Just how long this battle would have lasted I do not know, for at that moment he was relieved by an official who was as helpful as he had been hostile, as benign as he had been bellicose. Within three minutes the box and all my luggage had been loaded on to the waiting car and we were on the last lap of the journey. What meant still more to me was that from the box there now came a faint enquiring chitter and a rustle of wood shavings.

Mijbil had in fact displayed a characteristic shared, I believe, by many animals; an apparent step, as it were, on the road to travel-shock death, but in fact a powerful buffer against it. Many animals seem to me to be able to go into a deep sleep, a coma, almost, as a voluntary act independent of exhaustion; it is an escape mechanism that comes into operation when the animal's inventiveness in the face of adversity has failed to ameliorate its circumstances. I have seen it very occasionally in trapped animals; an arctic fox in Finmark, captive by the leg for no more than an hour, a badger in a Surrey wood, a common house mouse in a box trap. It is, of course, almost a norm, too, of animals kept in too cramped quarters in zoos and in pet stores. I came to recognize it later in Mij when he travelled in cars, a thing he hated; after a few minutes of frenzy he would curl himself into a tight ball and banish entirely the distasteful world about him.

On that first day that he arrived in England he had, I think, been in just such a barricaded state ever since the lid of the box was nailed down before reaching Paris; back, for all one may know, among the familiar scenes of his Tigris swamps, or perhaps in a negative, imageless world where the medulla had taken over respiration and the forebrain rested in a state bordering upon catalepsy.

He was wide awake once more by the time we reached my flat, and when I had the driver paid off and the door closed behind me I felt a moment of deep emotional satisfaction, almost of triumph, that I had after all brought back a live otter cub from Iraq to London, and that Camusfeàrna was less than six hundred miles distant from me.

I prised open the lid of the box, and Mijbil clambered out into my arms to greet me with a frenzy of affection that I felt I had hardly merited.

8

I LIVED at that time in a studio flat near to Olympia, one large room with a sleeping gallery that opened on to the garage roof, and penthouse premises at the back containing kitchen, bathroom and box-room, each of diminutive size and resembling a divided corridor. Despite the absence of a garden, these unconventional premises held certain advantages for an otter, for the garage roof eliminated the normal difficulties of keeping a house-trained animal in a London flat, and the box-room opening from the bathroom provided quarters in which at any time he might be left for short periods with all his essential requirements. But just how short those periods would be—a maximum of four or five hours—had never struck me until Mij had already become the centre point round which, eccentrically, revolved my life. Otters that have been reared by human beings demand human company, much affection, and constant co-operative play; without these things they quickly become unhappy, and for the most part they are tiresome in direct ratio to their discontent. They can be trying, too, out of sheer inquisitiveness and exuberance of spirits, but not in the seemingly calculated way that is born of deprivation.

The spacious tile-floored bedroom of the Consulate-General at Basra, with its minimum of inessential furniture or bric-à-brac, had done little to prepare me for the problems that my crowded and vulnerable studio would present in relation to Mijbil. Exhausted as he was that first night, he had not been out of his box for five minutes before he set out with terrifying enthusiasm to explore his new quarters. I had gone to the kitchen to find fish for him, expected by prearrangement with my charlady, but I had hardly got there before I heard the first crash of breaking china in the room behind me. The fish and the bath solved the problem temporarily, for when he had eaten he went wild with joy in the water and romped ecstatically for a full half hour, but it was clear that the flat would require considerable alteration if it was to remain a home for both of us. Meanwhile sleep seemed long overdue, and I saw only one solution; I laid a sleeping bag on the sofa, and anchored Mij to the sofa-leg by his lead.

I have never been able fully to make up my mind whether certain aspects of otter behaviour merely chance to resemble that of human beings, or whether, in the case of animals as young as Mij was, there is actual mimicry of the human foster parent. Mij, anyway, seemed to regard me closely as I composed myself on my back with a cushion under my head; then, with a confiding air of knowing exactly what to do, he clambered up beside me and worked his body down into the sleeping-bag until he lay flat on his back inside it with his head on the cushion beside mine and his fore-paws in the air. In this position, such an attitude as a child devises for its teddy-bear in bed, Mij heaved an enormous sigh and was instantly asleep.

There is, in fact, much about otters that encourages humans to a facile anthropomorphizing. A dry otter at play is an animal that might have been specifically designed to please a child; they look like 'invented' animals, and are really much more like Giovannetti's 'Max' than anything else, a comparison that has instantly struck many people upon seeing my otters for the first time—the same short legs, the same tubby, furry torso, vast whiskers, and clownish good humour. In the water they take on quite a different aspect and personality, supple as an eel, fast as lightning, and graceful as a ballet dancer, but very few people have watched them for long below the surface, and I have yet to see a zoo that gives its otters a glass-sided tank—a spectacle that I believe would steal the show from the whole aquarium.

Mij and I remained in London for nearly a month, while, as my landlord put it, the studio came to look like a cross between a monkey-house and a furniture repository. The garage roof was fenced in, and a wire gate fitted to the gallery stairs, so that he could occasionally be excluded from the studio itself; the upstairs telephone was enclosed in a box (whose fastening he early learned to undo); my dressing-table was cut off from him by a wire flap hinging from the ceiling, and the electric light wires were enclosed in tunnels of hardboard that gave the place the appearance of a power-house.

All these precautions were entirely necessary, for if Mij thought that he had been excluded for too long, more especially from visitors whose acquaintance he wished to make, he would set about laying waste with extraordinary invention. No amount of forethought that I could muster was ever able to forestall his genius; there was always something that I had overlooked, something that could be made to speak with a crash for his mood of frustration, and it did not take me long to learn that prophylaxis was more convenient than treatment.

There was nothing haphazard about the demonstrations he planned; into them went all the patience and ingenuity of his remarkable brain and all the agility of his muscular little body. One evening, for example, after the contractors had departed for the third or fourth time, leaving, as I thought, an otter-proof situation at last, I had confined Mij to the gallery for an hour in deference to the wishes of a female visitor who feared for her nylons. He appeared, after a few moments, balancing adroitly on the top of the gallery railing, paying no attention either to us or to the formidable drop below him, for his plan was evidently already mature. At various points along the length of this railing were suspended certain decorative objects, a Cretan shepherd's bag, a dagger, and other things whose identity now eludes me. Purposefully, and with an air of enormous self-satisfaction, Mij began to chew through the cords from which these *objets d'art* or *de voyage* hung. After each severance he would pause to watch his victim crash to the parquet floor below, then he would carefully renew his precarious, straddling progress along the rail until he reached the next. We stood, my visitor and I, waiting to catch the more fragile items as they fell, and I remember that when the last fruit, as it were, had fallen from the bough she turned to me with a sigh and said, 'Don't you ever feel that this just simply can't go on?'

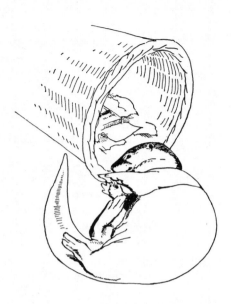

More usually, however, when he was loose in the studio, he would play for hours at a time with what soon became an established selection of toys, ping-pong balls, marbles, india-rubber fruit, and a terrapin shell that I had brought back from his native marshes. The smaller among these objects he became adept at throwing right across the room with a flick of his head, and with a ping-pong ball he invented a game of his own which would keep him engrossed for up to half an hour at a time. An expanding suitcase that I had taken to Iraq had become damaged on the journey home, so that the lid, when closed, remained at a slope from one end to the other. Mij discovered that if he placed the ball on the high end it would run down the length of the suitcase unaided. He would dash round to the other end to ambush its arrival, hide from it, crouching, to spring up and take it by surprise as it reached the drop to the floor, grab it and trot off with it to the high end once more.

These games were adequate for perhaps half of all the time he spent indoors and awake, but several times a day he needed, as much psychologically as physically, I think, a prolonged romp with a human playmate. Tunnelling under the carpet and affecting to believe himself thus rendered invisible, he would shoot out with a squeak of triumph if a foot passed within range; or he would dive inside the loose cover of the sofa and play tigers from behind it; or he would simply lay siege to one's person as a puppy does, bouncing around one in a frenzy of excited chirps and squeaks and launching a series of tip-and-run raids. It was the 'tip' that was the trouble, for his teeth were like needles, and however gently he might try to use them, such games used, I am bound to say, to end with a certain amount of visible proof of his success in tactics left on the human hand. It did not hurt, but it made a bad impression upon visitors, many of whom were ready in any case to accord him the distrust appropriate to an alien upstart.

But I soon found an infallible way to distract his attention if he became too excitable, a way whose success was, I think, due to the refusal to be baffled by obstacles that is an otter characteristic. I would take the terrapin shell, wrap it in a towel, and knot the loose ends tightly across. He came to know these preparations, and would wait absolutely motionless until I handed him the bundle; then he would straddle it with his fore-arms, sink his teeth in the knots, and begin to hump and shuffle round the room in a deceptively aimless-seeming manner. Deceptive, because no matter how complex the knots he would have them all undone in five or ten minutes. At the end of this performance he liked, and seemed to expect, applause, and he would then bring the towel and the terrapin shell to be tied up again. He brought the towel first, dragging it, and then made a second trip for the terrapin, shuffling it in front of him down the room like a football.

At night he slept in my bed, still, at this time, on his back with his head on the pillow, and in the morning he shared my bath. With utter indifference to temperature he would plunge ahead of me into water still too hot for me to enter, and while I shaved he would swim round me playing with the soapsuds or with various celluloid and rubber ducks and ships that had begun to accumulate in my bathroom as they do in a child's.

Outside the house I exercised him on a lead, precisely as if he had been a dog, and, like a dog, he soon showed preference for certain streets and certain corners at which dogs of all sorts and sizes had left stimulating messages; messages that were, perhaps, the more fascinating for being, as it were, in a foreign language. Whether or not he could decipher their purport, whether or not they conjured up for him the various erotic, impudent or pugnacious images intended, he would spend minutes at a time sniffing these clearing-houses of local canine information, and would occasionally add to them some liquid comment of his own, tantalisingly cryptic, no doubt, to the next comer.

I was too timid of the result to allow him to meet any dog so to speak nose to nose, and I would pick him up if we met unattended dogs in the street, but for his part he seemed largely indifferent to them. The only time that I was conscious of some mutual recognition taking place, some awareness of similarity between canine and lutrine values, was one morning when, setting out for his walk, he refused to be parted from a new toy, a large rubber ball painted in gaudy segments. This ball was too big for his mouth, so that he could only carry it sticking out from one side of his jaws like a gigantic gum boil, and thus encumbered he set off briskly up the street, tugging at his lead. Rounding the first street corner we came face to face with a very fat spaniel, unattended and sedately carrying in its mouth a bundle of newspapers. The respective loads of otter and dog made it difficult for either of them to turn its head far as they came abreast, but their eyes rolled sideways with what appeared to me a wild surmise, and when they were a few paces past each other both suddenly stopped dead for a moment, as though arrested by some momentary mental revelation.

Mij quickly developed certain compulsive habits on these walks in the London streets, akin, clearly, to the rituals of children who on their way to and from school must place their feet squarely on the centre of each paving block; must touch every seventh upright of the iron railings, or pass to the outside of every second lamp post. Opposite to my flat was a single-storied primary school, along whose frontage ran a low wall some two feet high separating a corridor-width strip of garden from the road. On his way home, but never on his way out, Mij would tug me in the direction of this wall, jump up on it, and gallop the full length of its thirty yards, to the hopeless distraction both of pupils and of staff within. There was more than one street of which he would use one pavement only, refusing with dug-in toes to be led to the other side, and there were certain drain grilles through which he would peer motionless for long seconds before he could be led away from them. On return to the flat he would scrabble frantically to be let in, and the moment his lead was unhitched he would roll on his back and squirm with eye-bewildering speed and vigour before returning to his toys.

Many of his actions, indeed, appeared ritual, and I think that comparatively few people who keep wild creatures realize the enormous security-value of routine in the maintenance of an animal's contentment. As soon as routine is broken a new element enters, in however minute and unrecognizable a trace—the fear of the unknown which is basic to the behaviour of all animals, including man. Every living creature exists by a routine of some kind; the small rituals of that routine are the landmarks, the boundaries of security, the reassuring walls that exclude a *horror vacui*; thus, in our own species, after some tempest of the spirit in which the landmarks seem to have been swept away, a man will reach out tentatively in mental darkness to feel the walls, to assure himself that they still stand where they stood—a necessary gesture, for the walls are of his own building, without universal reality, and what man makes he may destroy. To an animal these landmarks are of even greater importance, for once removed from its natural surroundings, its ecological norm, comparatively little of what the senses perceive can be comprehended in function or potentiality, and the true conditions for insecurity are already established. As among human beings, animal insecurity may manifest itself as aggression or timidity, ill-temper or ill-health, or as excessive affection for a parental figure; unfortunately this last aspect encourages many to cultivate insecurity in their charges, child or animal, as a means to an end.

It was about this time that Mij delivered his first serious, intentional bite. He was fed now upon live eels—which I had learned to be the staple food of many races of otter—supplemented by a mixture of raw egg and unpolished rice, a sticky concoction for which he evinced a gusto no doubt influenced by his early life among the Arabs. The eels I kept in a perforated bucket under the kitchen tap, and fed them to him in the bath; it had become an established way of quieting him when he was obstreperous, to shut him in with a full bath of water and three or four eels. On this occasion I had closed the bathroom door imperfectly, and Mij elected to bring his second eel through and eat it in the studio. To this, though he was sodden with water and the eel very slimy, there seemed no alternative, for it is folly to try to take away from a wild animal its natural prey; but when after a few mouthfuls he decided to carry it upstairs to the gallery I determined to call a halt, visualizing a soaking and eel-slimed bed. I put on three pairs of gloves, the outermost being a pair of heavily-padded flying gauntlets. I caught up with him half-way up the stairway; he laid down the eel, put a paw on it, and hummed at me, a high continuous hum that could break out into a wail. Full of euphoric self confidence I talked away quietly to him, telling him that he couldn't possibly hurt me and that I was going to take the eel back to the bathroom. The humming became much louder. I bent down and put my heavily-gloved hand upon the eel. He screamed at me, but still he took no action. Then, as I began to lift it, he bit. He bit just once and let go; the canines of his upper and lower jaws passed through the three layers of glove, through the skin, through muscle and bone, and met in the middle of my hand with an audible crunch. He let go almost in the same instant, and rolled on his back squirming with apology. I still held the eel; I carried it back to the bath, where he refused to pay any further attention to it, fussing round me and over me and muzzling me with little squeals of affection and apparent solicitude.

There were two small bones broken in my hand, and for a week it was the size of a boxing glove, very painful, and an acute embarrassment to me in the presence of those who from the first had been sceptical of Mij's domesticity. I had been given a sharp and necessary reminder that though he might carry painted rubber balls through the London streets he was not a spaniel.

It was not lack of curiosity, so much as lack of time and opportunity, that made me delay for nearly three weeks before making any real effort to establish Mij's identity. It would, I thought, require a day's research in the library of the Zoological Society, and at that early stage Mij could not be left alone for more than an hour or so without fretting. But, as may be imagined, he caused no small stir in his walks through the streets of West Kensington, and it was increasingly borne in upon me that I could answer only in the most perfunctory and unsatisfactory terms the fire of questions with which our strolls were punctuated.

It is not, I suppose, in any way strange that the average Londoner should not recognize an otter, but the variety of guesses as to what kind of animal this might be came as no less of a surprise to me than the consistent accuracy with which a minority bracketed the bull's-eye without once touching it. Otters belong to a comparatively small group of animals called Mustellines, shared by the badger, mongoose, weasel, stoat, polecat, marten, mink and others; the official at Cairo airport had set an early precedent of outer scoring when he asked whether Mij was an ermine—which is, of course, a stoat in winter coat. Now, in the London streets, I faced a continual barrage of conjectural questions that sprayed all the Mustellines but the otter; wilder, more random fire hit on practically everything from 'a baby seal' to a squirrel. The seal heresy had deep root, and was perhaps the commonest of them all, though far from being the most bizarre; 'Is that a walrus, mister?' reduced me to giggles outside Harrods, and 'a hippo' made my day outside Cruft's Dog Show. A beaver, a bear cub, a newt, a leopard—one, apparently, that had changed his spots—even, with heaven knows what dim recollections of schoolroom science and a bewildering latinized world of sub-human creatures—a 'brontosaur'; Mij was anything but an otter.

But the question for which I awarded the highest score—a question evading with contemptuous dexterity any possible inaccuracy on the part of the speaker; putting the blame, as it were, for the creature's unfamiliarity squarely on my own shoulders; hinting, or doing more than hint, that someone had blundered, that the hand of the potter had shaken; containing, too,

108

Mijbil in a glass tank.
Drawings by Michael Ayrton

an accusation of unfinished work unfit for exhibition—came from a Herculean labourer engaged, mightily and alone, upon digging a hole in the street. I was still far from him when he laid down his pick, put his hands on his hips, and began to stare. As I drew nearer I saw that this stare held an outraged quality, one of surprise, certainly, but also of affront, as though he would have me know that he was not one upon whom to play jokes. I came abreast of him; he spat, glared, and then growled out, ' 'Ere, mister—*what is that supposed to be?*'

It was, I think, his question more than any other that reminded me of my own ignorance; I did not, in fact, know what Mij was supposed to be. I knew, certainly, that he was an otter, but I also knew that he must be one of a species which, if known to the scientific world, was at least not known to live in the delta marshes of the Tigris and Euphrates, for the scant zoological literature that had accompanied me to Iraq made it plain that the only known otter of the Mesopotamian marshes was the Persian sub-species of the common European otter, *Lutra lutra*. Chahala, the cub that had died, had clearly belonged to that race; she had longer fur with 'guard hairs' in place of Mij's sleek, darker velvet; she was lighter on her throat and belly than upon her back, whereas Mij's body seemed to have been slipped into an evenly-dyed plush bag; the under side of her tail was not, as was Mij's, flat like a ruler.

In a village of the marshes between the Tigris and the Persian frontier I had bought two otter skins from the householder with whom we had been staying; both were, apart from any possible scientific interest, objects of fascination, for they had been 'case' skinned, the whole carcase having been removed, without a single incision, through the mouth. One of these skins belonged to Chahala's race; the other, contrast heightened by juxtaposition, was plainly of Mij's, a much larger and darker creature, whose fur was short and shiny and the colour of milkless chocolate. These two skins now reposed in my flat, pregnant with possibility and as yet unexamined by competent authority.

I telephoned to the Natural History department of the British Museum, in Cromwell Road, and the same afternoon Mr. Robert

Hayman arrived at my flat to examine the two skins and the living specimen. There is in the serious zoological world a dead-pan-ness, an unwillingness for committal, that must rival the most cautious of consulting physicians. Hayman was far too competent a zoologist, far too encyclopedic in his knowledge, to have been unaware in those first moments that he was looking at a skin and a living animal from a habitat that made the race quite unfamiliar to him, but he did not betray it. He took such measurements as Mij would permit, examined him closely, peered at his formidable array of teeth, and left bearing the two skins for comparison with museum series.

But in due course, after the slow, precise, painstaking processes of the taxonomic world, Mij's new race was proclaimed. Hayman summoned me to the museum to see the cabinets of otter skins from all over Asia, where the larger of mine lay, unlabelled and conspicuously differing from any other, in a drawer by itself, but in apposition to its nearest relatives. These, various sub-species of *Lutrogale*, a short-coated otter with a flat under side to the tail, ranged over most of Eastern Asia; according to their geographical race they were of a variety of hues from pale sandy to medium brown, but none had been recorded west of Sind, in India, and none resembled my specimens in colour.

There are very few people, and even fewer amateur zoologists, who stumble upon a sizeable mammal previously unknown to science; in the nursery world of picture-books of birds and beasts the few who had given their own names to species—Steller's Eider and Sea Eagle, Sharpe's Crow, Humboldt's Woolly Monkey, Meinerzthagen's Forest Hog, Ross's Snow Goose, Grant's Gazelle, Père David's Deer—had been surrounded for me with an aura of romance; they were the creators, partaking a little of the deity, who had contributed to the great panorama of bright living creatures in which, unshadowed and uncomplicated by know-ledge, my childish fancy wandered. Now, when Hayman suggested that the new otter should bear my name, I experienced a sharp, brief conflict; I felt that it should bear his, for he, not I, had done the work; but something small and shrill from the nursery days was shouting inside me that I could be translated into the hierarchy of my early gods and wear, however perilously, the halo of a creator. ('Can I have it for my own?' we used to ask when we were small. 'For my *very* own?' Here, surely, was an animal of my very own, to bear my name; every animal that looked like it would always bear my name for ever and ever, unless some odious taxonomist of the future, some leveller, some jealous, dusty scribe of the backroom and the skeletons, were to plot against me and plan the destruction of my tiny, living memorial.)

So Mij and all his race became *Lutrogale perspicillata maxwelli*, and though he is now no more, and there is no ostensible proof that there is another living specimen in the world, I had realized a far-off childish fantasy, and there was a Maxwell's otter.

9

IT WAS now early May, and I had been in London for more than three weeks, three weeks of impatience and nostalgia for Camus-feàrna, and I felt I could wait no longer to see Mij playing, as I visualized him, under the waterfall, or free about the burn and the island beaches. I went by way of my family home in the south of Scotland, where Mij could taste a partial but' guarded liberty before emancipation to total freedom in the north.

Travelling with otters is a very expensive business. There was now no question of again confining Mij to a box, and there is, unfortunately, no other legitimate means of carrying an otter by train. For the illegitimate means which I followed then and after, I paid, as do all who have recourse to black markets, highly. He travelled with me in a first-class sleeper, a form of transport which for some reason he enjoyed hugely; indeed from the very first he showed a perverse predilection for railway stations, and a total disregard for their deafening din and alarming crowd scenes.

At the barrier the railway official punched for me a dog ticket (on which I had noticed the words 'Give full Description') and had already turned to the next in the queue before his eyes widened in a perfect double take; then Mij was tugging up the crowded platform at the end of his lead, heedless of the shouts and the bustle, the screaming train hooters and rumbling luggage trolleys.

I had planned this operation with some care, visualizing each hazard and circumventing it as far as possible in advance; my hush money was already paid; the basket I carried contained everything conceivably necessary to Mij for the journey; over my left arm was an army blanket ready to protect the sheets from Mij's platform-grimed paws as soon as he entered the sleeper. When the initial penetration of the citadel, as it were, passed off without the slightest hitch, I felt that I had reaped no more than the just rewards of my forethought.

Mij had an instant eye for anything connected with water, and the most cursory inspection of the sleeping compartment convinced him that in the wash basin, however dry at the moment, lay the greatest pleasure-potential; he curled up in it, his form fitting its contours as an apple fits a dumpling, and his paws began increasingly feverish experiments with the chromium tap. It was, however, of a type entirely new to him, operating by downward pressure, and not a drop could he draw from it for a full five minutes; at last, trying to lever himself into an upright position, he put his full weight on the tap handle and found himself, literally, in his element.

There was only one incident that evening, an incident, however, that for a moment bade fair to bring the whole train to a stop and to expose to the outraged eyes of officialdom my irregular travelling companion. My attention had wandered from Mij; the train was roaring up through the Midlands in summer dusk, and I was watching out of the window the green corn and the black-thorn hedges and the tall trees heavy with leaf, and thinking how effectively the glass and the movement of the train insulated one from any intimacy with these desirable things while seeming to offer no protection against the impact of drab industrial land-scapes. Thus occupied, it had not occurred to me that Mij could, in that very confined space, get into any serious mischief; it had not crossed my mind, for example, that by standing on the piled luggage he could reach the communication cord. This, however, was precisely what he had done, and when my eye lit on him he already had it firmly between his teeth while exploring with his paws the tunnel into which its ends disappeared. It was probably nothing but this insatiable curiosity as to detail that had so far saved the situation; now as I started towards him he removed his fingers from the recess and braced them against the wall for the tug. It takes a surprisingly strong pull to ring the communication bell (I have once done so, when the only other passenger in my compartment died while lighting his pipe), but Mij had the necessary strength, and, it seemed, the determination. I caught him round the shoulders, but he retained his grip, and as I pulled him I saw the chain bulge ominously outward; I changed my tactics and pushed him towards it, but he merely braced his arms afresh. It seemed a deadlock, and one that might end in ignominy, until suddenly inspiration came to me. Mij was extremely ticklish, particularly over the region of the ribs. I began to tickle him feverishly, and at once his jaws relaxed into the foolish grin that he reserved for such occasions and he began to squirm. Later that evening he tried several times to reach the cord again, but by then I had redisposed the suitcases, and it was beyond the furthest stretch of his elastic body.

It was in unfamiliar surroundings such as these that Mij appeared most often to copy my actions; that night, though by now he had become accustomed to sleep inside the bed with his head to my feet, he arranged himself as he had on the first night at my flat, on his back with his head on the pillow and his arms outside the bedclothes. He was still so disposed when the attendant brought my tea in the morning. He stared at Mij, and said, 'Was it tea for one, or two, sir?'

During his stay at Monreith, the home of my family, Mij's character began to emerge and to establish itself. At first on farm mill dams, then in the big loch over which the house looks out, and finally in the sea—which, though he had never known salt water, he entered without apparent surprise—he demonstrated not only his astonishing swimming powers but his willingness to reject the call of freedom in favour of human company. At first, guessing the urgency of the summons that his instincts would experience, I allowed him to swim only on the end of a long fishing line. I had bought a spring reel, which automatically took up the slack, and attached this to the butt end of a salmon rod, but the danger of underwater snags on which the line might loop itself soon seemed too great, and after the first week he ran free and swam free. He wore a harness to which a lead could be attached in emergency, but its function was as much to proclaim his domesticity to would-be human aggressors as one of restraint. The design of this harness, one that would neither impede movement nor catch upon submerged branches and drown him, was a subject that occupied my imagination for many months, and was not perfected for nearly a year.

This time of getting to know a wild animal on terms, as it were, of mutual esteem, was wholly fascinating to me, and our long daily walks by stream and hedgerow, moorland and loch, were a source of perpetual delight. Though it remained difficult to lure him from some enticing piece of open water, he was otherwise no more trouble than a dog, and infinitely more interesting to watch. His hunting powers were still undeveloped, but he would sometimes corner an eel in the mill dams, and in the streams he would catch frogs, which he skinned with a dexterity seemingly born of long practice. I had rightly guessed that his early life in a Marsh Arab household would have produced an enlightened and progressive attitude towards poultry—for no Ma'dan would tolerate a predator among the sparse and scrawny scarecrows that pass in the marshes for chickens—and in fact I found that Mij would follow me through a crowded and cackling farmyard without a glance to right or to left. To most domestic livestock he was indifferent, but black cattle he clearly identified with the water buffaloes of his home, and if they gathered at the edge of water in which he was swimming he became wild with excitement, plunging and porpoising and chittering with pleasure.

Even in the open countryside he retained his passion for playthings, and would carry with him for miles some object that had caught his fancy, a fallen rhododendron blossom, an empty twelve-bore cartridge case, a fir-cone, or, on one occasion, a woman's comb with an artificial brilliant set in the bar; this he discovered at the side of the drive as we set off one morning, and carried it for three hours, laying it down on the bank when he took to water and returning for it as soon as he emerged.

In the traces left by wild otters he took not the slightest interest. Following daily the routes for which Mij expressed preference, I found myself almost imperceptibly led by his instinct into the world in which the otters of my own countryside lived, a watery world of deep-cut streams between high, rooty banks where the leaves of the undergrowth met overhead; of unguessed alleys and tunnels in reedbeds by a loch's edge; of mossy culverts and marsh-marigolds; of islands tangled with fallen trees among whose roots were earthy excavations and a whisper of the wind in the willows. As one may hear or read a strange, unusual name, and thereafter be haunted by its constant coincidental recurrence, so, now that I had through Mijbil become conscious of otters, I saw all around me the signs of their presence where I had been oblivious to them before; a smoothed bank of steep mud which they had used for toboganning; a hollowed-out rotten tree-stump whose interior had been formed into a dry sleeping place; the print of a broad, capable, webbed foot; a small tarry dropping, composed mainly of eel-bones, deposited upon a stone in midstream. In these last I had expected Mij to show at least an equal interest to that which he had displayed in their canine counterparts, but whether because otters do not use their excreta in an anecdotal or informative way, or because he did not recognize in these the product of his own kind, he treated them as if they did not exist.

During all the time that I had him he killed, so far as I know, only one warm-blooded animal, and then he did not eat it, for he seemed to have a horror of blood and of the flesh of warm-blooded animals. On this occasion he was swimming in a reedy loch when he caught a moorhen chick of a few days old, a little black gollywog of a creature half the size of a day-old chick. He had a habit of tucking his treasures under one arm when he was swimming—for an otter swimming under-water uses its fore-limbs very little—and here he placed the chick while he went on in a leisurely way with his underwater exploration. It must have drowned during the first minute or so, and when at length he brought it ashore for a more thorough investigation he appeared disappointed and irritated by this unwarrantable fragility; he nuzzled it and pushed it about with his paws and chittered at it in a pettish sort of way, and then, convinced of its now permanent inertia, he left it where it lay and went in search of something more co-operative.

In the library at Monreith I explored what natural historians of earlier generations had to say about otters. There were no recent works, for the relevant section of the library had received no addition for many years past. That garrulous eighteenth-century clown the Comte de Buffon, whose nineteen volumes had acquired a petulant flavour by his contemporary translator's insistence on the use of the English word 'pretend' for the French *prétendre*, did not, on the whole, approve of otters. He was a whimsical man, much concerned with the curious, and credulous as to the existence of most patently improbable creatures, which he himself tried assiduously to produce by arranging monstrous matings (after much experiment he was disappointedly forced to the conclusion that a bull and a mare 'could copulate neither with pleasure nor profit'); furthermore he appeared to attach some mystic significance to whether an animal could or could not be persuaded to eat honey. Otters, he found, could not.

'Young animals are generally beautiful; but the young otter is not so handsome as the old. A head ill shaped, ears placed low, eyes small and covered, a lurid aspect, awkward motions, an ignoble and deformed figure, and a kind of mechanical cry, which he repeats every moment, seem to indicate a stupid animal. The otter, however, acquires industry with age, sufficient, at least, to carry on a successful war against the fishes, who, both with regard to sentiment and instinct, are much inferior to other animals. But I can hardly allow him to have the talents of the beaver. . . . All I know is, that the otters dig no habitations for themselves, . . . that they often change their places of abode; that they banish their young at the end of six weeks or two months; that those I attempted to tame endeavoured to bite; that some days after they became more gentle, perhaps because they were weak or sick; that, so far from being easily accustomed to a domestic life, all of them that I attempted to bring up, died young; that the otter is naturally of a cruel and savage disposition. . . . His retreats exhale a noxious odour, from the remains of putrid fishes; and his own body has a bad smell. The flesh is extremely fishy and disagreeable. The Romish Church permits the use of it on maigre days. In the kitchen of the Carthusian convent, near Dijon, Mr. Pennant saw one preparing for the dinner of the religious of the rigid order, who, by their rules, are prohibited, during their whole lives, the eating of flesh.'

This description might perhaps have proved somewhat discouraging had I not such abundant first-hand evidence to refute it, but if Buffon had been the otter's principal detractor, the great American naturalist a Ernest Thompson Seton was certainly champion in chief. Writing soon after the turn of this century he said, 'Of all the beasts whose lives I have tried to tell, there is one that stands forth, the Chevalier Bayard of the wilds—without fear and without reproach. That is the otter, the joyful, keen, and fearless otter; mild and loving to his own kind, and gentle with his neighbour of the stream; full of play and gladness in his life, full of courage in his stress; ideal in his home, steadfast in death; the noblest little soul that ever went four-footed through the woods.' In his writings I recognized the animal that I knew, 'the most beautiful and engaging of all elegant pets. There seems no end to its fun, its energy, its drollery, its good nature, and its postures of new and surprising grace. I never owned a pet otter, but I never yet saw one without shamelessly infringing article number ten of the Decalogue.'[1] While noting that in its structural affinities 'the otter is nothing but a big water weasel' he adds, writing of the toboganing habit. 'It is a delightful proof of growth and uplift when we find an adult animal setting aside a portion of its time and effort for amusement, and especially for social amusement. A large number of the noblest animals thus relax from sordid life and pursue amusement with time and applicances after a fashion that finds its highest development in man.'

Yet another early writer, whose name I find elusive, remarked, with a certain quaint charm in choice of words that 'the Otter is of course a giant amphibious stoat whose nature has been softened by the gentling and ennobling influence of the fisher life.'

We arrived at Camusfeàrna in early June, soon after the beginning of a long spell of Mediterranean weather. My diary tells me that summer begins on 22nd June, and under the heading

[1] *Life Histories of Northern Animals* (Constable, 1910).

for 24th June there is a somewhat furtive aside to the effect that it is Midsummer's day, as though to ward off the logical deduction that summer lasts only for four days in every year. But that summer at Camusfeàrna seemed to go on and on through timeless hours of sunshine and stillness and the dapple of changing cloud shadow upon the shoulders of the hills.

When I think of early summer at Camusfeàrna a single enduring image comes forward through the multitude that jostle in kaleidoscopic patterns before my mind's eye—that of wild roses against a clear blue sea, so that when I remember that summer alone with my curious namesake who had travelled so far, those roses have become for me the symbol of a whole complex of peace. They are not the pale, anaemic flowers of the south, but a deep, intense pink that is almost a red; it is the only flower of that colour, and it is the only flower that one sees habitually against the direct background of the ocean, free from the green stain of summer. The yellow flag irises flowering in dense ranks about the burn and the foreshore, the wild orchids bright among the heather and mountain grasses, all these lack the essential contrast, for the eye may move from them to the sea beyond them only through the intermediary, as it were, of the varying greens among which they grow. It is in June and October that the colours at Camusfeàrna run riot, but in June one must face seaward to escape the effect of wearing green-tinted spectacles. There at low tide the rich ochres, madders and oranges of the orderly strata of seaweed species are set against glaring, vibrant whites of barnacle-covered rock and shell sand, with always beyond them the elusive, changing blues and purples of the moving water, and somewhere in the foreground the wild roses of the north.

Into this bright, watery landscape Mij moved and took possession with a delight that communicated itself as clearly as any articulate speech could have done; his alien but essentially appropriate entity occupied and dominated every corner of it, so that he became for me the central figure among the host of wild creatures with which I was surrounded. The waterfall, the burn, the white beaches and the islands; his form became the familiar foreground to them all—or perhaps foreground is not the right

word, for at Camusfeàrna he seemed so absolute a part of his surroundings that I wondered how they could ever have seemed to
me complete before his arrival.

At the beginning, while I was still imbued with the caution and
forethought that had so far gone to his tending, Mij's daily life
followed something of a routine; this became, as the weeks went
on, relaxed into a total freedom at the centre point of which
Camusfeàrna house remained Mij's holt, the den to which he
returned at night, and in the daytime when he was tired. But this
emancipation, like most natural changes, took place so gradually
and unobtrusively that it was difficult for me to say at what point
the routine had stopped.

Mij slept in my bed (by now, as I have said, he had abandoned
the teddy-bear attitude and lay on his back under the bedclothes
with his whiskers tickling my ankles and his body at the crook
of my knees) and would wake with bizarre punctuality at exactly
twenty past eight in the morning. I have sought any possible
explanation for this, and some 'feed-back' situation in which it
was actually I who made the first unconscious movement, giving
him his cue, cannot be altogether discounted; but whatever the
reason, his waking time, then and until the end of his life, summer
or winter, remained precisely twenty past eight. Having woken,
he would come up to the pillow and nuzzle my face and neck
with small attenuated squeaks of pleasure and affection. If I did
not rouse myself very soon he would set about getting me out of
bed. This he did with the business-like, slightly impatient
efficiency of a nurse dealing with a difficult child. He played the
game by certain defined and self-imposed rules; he would not,
for example, use his teeth even to pinch, and inside these limitations it was hard to imagine how a human brain could, in the
same body, have exceeded his ingenuity. He began by going
under the bedclothes and moving rapidly up and down the bed
with a high-hunching, caterpillar-like motion that gradually un-
tucked the bedclothes from beneath the sides of the mattress; this
achieved he would redouble his efforts at the foot of the bed,
where the sheets and blankets had a firmer hold. When everything had been loosened up to his satisfaction he would flow off

the bed on to the floor—except when running on dry land the only appropriate word for an otter's movement is flowing; they pour themselves, as it were, in the direction of their objective—take the bedclothes between his teeth, and, with a series of violent tugs, begin to yank them down beside him. Eventually, for I do not wear pyjamas, I would be left quite naked on the undersheet, clutching the pillows rebelliously. But they, too, had to go; and it was here that he demonstrated the extraordinary strength concealed in his small body. He would work his way under them and execute a series of mighty hunches of his arched back, each of them lifting my head and whole shoulders clear of the bed, and at some point in the procedure he invariably contrived to dislodge the pillows while I was still in mid-air, much as a certain type of practical joker will remove a chair upon which someone is in the act of sitting down. Left thus comfortless and bereft both of covering and of dignity, there was little option but to dress, while Mij looked on with an all-that-shouldn't-really-have-been-necessary-you-know sort of expression. Otters usually get their own way in the end; they are not dogs, and they co-exist with humans rather than being owned by them.

His next objective was the eel-box in the burn, followed, having breakfasted, by a tour of the water perimeter, the three-quarter circle formed by the burn and the sea; shooting like an under-water arrow after trout where the burn runs deep and slow between the trees; turning over stones for hidden eels where it spreads broad and shallow over sun-reflecting scales of mica; tobogganing down the long, loose sand slope by the sand-martin colony; diving through the waves on the sand beach and catching dabs; then, lured in with difficulty and subterfuge from starting on a second lap, home to the kitchen and ecstatic squirming among his towels.

This preamble to the day, when Mij had a full stomach and I had not, became, as he established favoured pools and fishing grounds which had every morning to be combed as for a lost possession, ever longer and longer, and after the first fortnight I took, not without misgiving, to going back indoors myself as soon as he had been fed. At first he would return after an hour or so, and when he had dried himself he would creep up under the loose cover of the sofa and form a round breathing hump at the centre of the seat. But as time went on he stayed longer about the burn, and I would not begin to worry until he had been gone for half the day.

There were great quantities of cattle at Camusfeàrna that year, for the owner of the estate was of an experimental turn of mind, and had decided to farm cattle on the lines of the Great Glen Cattle Ranch. The majority of these beasts were black, and, as at Monreith in the spring, Mij seemed to detect in them an affinity to his familiar water buffaloes of the Tigris marshes, for he would dance round them with excited chitterings until they stampeded. Thus massed they presented too formidable an appearance for him, and after a week or two he devised for himself a means of cattle-baiting at which he became a past master. With extreme stealth he would advance *ventre à terre* towards the rear end of some massive stirk whose black-tufted tail hung invitingly within his reach; then, as one who makes a vigorous and impatient tug at a bell-rope, he would grab the tuft between his teeth and give one tremendous jerk upon it with all his strength, leaping backward exactly in time to dodge the lashing hooves. At first I viewed this sport with the gravest alarm, for, owing to the structure of the skull, a comparatively light blow on the nose can kill an otter, but Mij was able to gauge the distance to an inch, and never a hoof so much as grazed him. As a useful by-product of his impish sense of humour, the cattle tended to keep farther from the house, thus incidentally reducing the number of scatological hazards to be skirted at the door.

I had a book to write during those summer months at Camusfeàrna, and often I would lie for hours in the sun by the waterfall; from time to time Mij would appear from nowhere, bounding up the bank from the water, to greet me as though we had been separated for weeks.

There is a patron saint of otters, St. Cuthbert—the eider duck, too, shares his patronage; clearly he was a man who bestowed his favours with the most enlightened discrimination—and there exists an eye-witness account of his converse with them.

'It was his way for the most part to wander in those places and to preach in those remote hamlets, perched on steep rugged mountain sides, where other men would have a dread of going, and whose poverty and rude ignorance gave no welcome to any scholar. . . . Often for a whole week, sometimes for two or three, and even for a full month, he would not return home, but would abide in the mountains, and call these simple folk to heavenly things by his word and his ways. . . .

'(*He was, moreover, easily entreated, and came to stay at the abbey of Coldingham on a cliff above the sea.*)

'As was his habit, at night while other men took their rest, he would go out to pray: and after long vigils kept far into the night, he would come home when the hour of common prayer drew near. One night, a brother of this same monastery saw him go silently out, and stealthily followed on his track, to see where he was going or what he would do. And so he went out from the monastery and, his spy following him, went down to the sea, above which the monastery was built: and wading into the depths till the waves swelled up to his neck and arms, kept his vigil through the dark with chanting voiced like the sea. As the twilight of dawn drew near, he waded back up the beach, and kneeling there, again began to pray: and as he prayed, straight from the depths of the sea came two four-footed beasts which are called by the common people otters. These, prostrate before him on the sand, began to busy themselves warming his feet with pantings, and trying to dry them with their fur; and when this good office was rendered, and they had his benediction they slipped back again beneath their native waters. He himself returned home, and sang the hymns of the office with the brethren at the appointed hour. But the brother who had stood watching him from the cliffs was seized with such panic that he could hardly make his way home, tottering on his feet: and early in the morning came to him and fell at his feet, begging forgiveness with his tears for his foolish attempt, never doubting but that his behaviour of the night was known and discovered.

'To whom Cuthbert: "What ails you, my brother? What have you done? Have you been out and about to try to come at the truth of this night wandering of mine? I forgive you, on this one condition: that you promise to tell no man what you saw, until my death." And the promise given, he blessed the brother and absolved him alike of the fault and the annoyance his foolish boldness had given: and the brother kept silence on the piece of valour that he had seen, until after the saint's death, when he took pains to tell it to many.'[1]

Now it is apparent to me that whatever other saintly virtues St. Cuthbert possessed he well merited canonization by reason of his forbearance alone. I know all about being dried by otters. I have been dried by them more times than I care to remember. Like everything else about otters, it takes place the wrong way round, so to speak. When one plays ball with a puppy, one throws the ball and the puppy fetches it back and then one throws it again; it is all comparatively restful and orderly. But when one plays ball with an otter the situation gets out of hand from the start; it is the otter who throws the ball—to a remarkable distance —and the human who fetches it. With the human who at the beginning is not trained to this the otter is fairly patient, but persistent and obstinate refusal meets with reprisals. The same upside-down situation obtains when being dried by otters. The otter emerges tempestuously from the sea or the river or the bath, as the case may be, carrying about half a gallon of water in its fur, and sets about drying you with a positively terrifying zeal and enthusiasm. Every inch of you requires, in the view of a conscientious otter, careful attention. The otter uses its back as the principal towel, and lies upon it while executing a series of vigorous, eel-like wriggles. In a surprisingly short space of time the otter is quite dry except for the last four inches of its tail, and the human being is soaking wet except for nothing. It is no use going to change one's clothes; in a few minutes the otter will come rampaging out of the water again intent upon its mission of drying people.

I have but little doubt what the good brother of Coldingham monastery really saw. St. Cuthbert had been praying at the water's edge, not, as the brother thought (it was, one must bear in mind,

[1] Helen Waddell, *Beasts and Saints* (Constable, 1934).

125

night, and the light was poor) up to his neck in the waves; and it was entirely the condition of the saint's clothing after he had been dried by the otters that led the observer to deduce some kind of sub-marine devotion. Clearly, too, it was an absolution rather than a simple benediction that the now shivering and bedraggled saint bestowed upon his tormentors. In the light of my interpretation St. Cuthbert's injunction to silence falls neatly into place, for he could not know of the brother's misapprehension, and not even a saint enjoys being laughed at in this kind of misfortune.

While otters undoubtedly have a special vocation for drying human beings they will also dry other objects, most particularly beds, between the sheets, all the way from the pillows to the bed-foot. A bed dried by this process is unusable for a week, and an otter-dried sofa is only tolerable in the heat of summer. I perceive why St. Cuthbert required the ministrations of the eider ducks and the warm down of their breasts; the unfortunate man must have been constantly threatened with an occupational pneumonia.

This aspect of life with an otter had never really struck me before I brought Mij to Camusfeàrna; in London one could run the water out of the bath, and by using a monster towel could render him comparatively harmless before he reached the sitting-room, while at Monreith the loch was far enough from the house for him to be dry before reaching home. But at Camusfeàrna, with the sea a stone's throw on one side and the burn on the other, I have found no satisfactory solution beyond keeping the bedroom door closed, and turning, as it were, a blind posterior to wet sofas and chairs.

The manuscript that I was writing that summer became blurred and stained as though by tears; I would lie, as I have said, sunbathing and writing in the grass by the burn, and every now and again Mij's busy quartering of the stream's bed from the falls to the sea and back again would bring him to the point above which I lay. With delighted squeaks and gurgles he would rush through the shallows and come bounding up the bank to deposit his skin-load of water indiscriminately upon myself and my manuscript, sometimes adding insult to injury by confiscating my pen as he departed.

In the sea, Mij discovered his true, breath-taking aquabatic powers; until he came to Scotland he had never swum in deep waters, for the lakes and lagoons of his native marshes are rarely more than a fathom or two deep. He would swim beside me as I rowed in the little dinghy, and in the glass-clear waters of Camusfeàrna bay, where the white shell sand alternates with sea tangle and outcrops of rock, I could watch him as he dived down, down, down through fathom after fathom to explore the gaudy sea forests at the bottom with their flowered shell glades and mysterious, shadowed caverns. He was able, as are all otters and seals, to walk on the bottom without buoyancy, for an otter swims habitually under water and does not dive with full lungs, depending for oxygen—we must presume in the absence of knowledge—upon a special adaptation of the venous system. The longest that I ever timed Mij below the surface was almost six minutes, but I had the impression that he was in no way taxing his powers, and could greatly have exceeded that time in emergency. Normally, however, if he was not engrossed, he would return to the surface every minute or so, breaking it for only a second, with a forward diving roll like that of a porpoise. Swimming at the surface, as he did if he wanted to keep some floating object in view, he was neither very fast nor graceful, a labouring dog-paddle in amazing contrast to his smooth darting grace below water. For hours he would keep pace with the boat, appearing now on this side and now on that, sometimes mischievously seizing an oar with both arms and dragging on it, and from time to time bouncing inboard with a flurry of water, momentarily recalled to his mission of drying people.

Only when I was fishing did I have to leave Mij shut up in the house, for he was a creature who must test everything with his mouth, and my worst nightmare was the vision of a mackerel hook in his jaw. At first I fished little, having no great liking for the lythe and coal fish that are all one may depend upon in early summer round the Camusfeàrna skerries. Though by mid-June there are all the signs of summer; the teeming, clangorous bird life of the islands established for many weeks and the samphire and goose-grass alive with downy chicks, it is not until July that with the coming of the mackerel the sea appears to burst into life; for following them come all the greater creatures that prey upon them, and the mackerel in their turn force up to the surface the lesser fishes upon which they feed, the small, glittering, multitudinous fry of many species, including their own. When far out on the blank face of the summer sea there are screaming patches of gulls that dip and swoop, half running, half flying, alighting with wings still open to grab and to swallow, one may guess that somewhere beneath them lies a great shoal of mackerel, who are pushing up to the surface and the waiting gulls the little fish fleeing in panic from, perhaps, their own parents. Sometimes there are curiously local patches of fry at the surface, and at sunset when the sea is really as smooth as glass—a much misused simile, for it rarely is—I have seen, miles from shore, little dancing foot-wide fountains of blue and silver mackerel no longer than a man's thumb, and have found no predator below them.

After the mackerel had arrived I fished for a few minutes in the cool of every evening; for them Mij, though he never caught one himself, so far as I knew, had an insatiable passion, as had Jonnie before him; and I too welcomed them, perhaps because of childhood associations. When I was a child in Galloway we used to fish for mackerel by trolling from a sailing-boat a single hook baited with bright metal, or with a sliver of flesh and skin sliced from a mackerel's flank (how well I recall the horror of seeing for the first time this operation performed upon the living fish; the tears, the reassurance, all among the blue waves and the spindrift and the flapping brown sail). We caught our fish singly and rebaited the hook each time, and if we caught twenty or thirty fish in an afternoon we chattered about it for weeks. It was not, I think, until shortly before the war that the murderous darrow came into general use in the West Highlands, and at Camusfeàrna, where there is no means of disposing of surplus fish but dumping them, it has the disadvantage of limiting fishing time to a few minutes. A darrow consists of a twelve-foot cast carrying up to twenty-two flies of crudely-dyed hen's feathers, weighted at the bottom with a two-pound sinker. The boat is stationary in anything from six to twenty fathoms of water, and the darrow and line are allowed to run out until the sinker bumps the bottom. By that time, as often as not in Camusfeàrna bay, there are half a dozen or so mackerel on the hooks. If there are not, it is simply a question of hauling in two fathoms of line and letting it run out again, and repeating this process until either the boat drifts over a shoal or a moving shoal happens to pass beneath the boat. Sometimes the mackerel are in shallower water, clear water where one can see fathoms down to pale sand and dark sea-tangle and rushing shoals of aquamarine fish as they dart at the bright feathers. Quite often every single fly is taken at once; then at one moment the line is lead-heavy, tugging and jerking, and at the next light as floating string as the mackerel swim upward carrying the sinker with them. There is a great art in dealing with a full darrow, for twenty-two large fish-hooks flipping wildly about the hold of a small boat catch more than fish. In the days of the Soay Shark Fishery I saw many barbs sunk deep in hands and legs of mackerel fishers; there was only one way of extraction, and a very painful one it was—to push the hook clean through, as opposed to pulling on it, then to snip off the barb with wire cutters and work the hook all the way back again.

It is not always mackerel that take the darrow flies; there are saith and lythe and the strangely heraldic gurnards, so fantastically armoured with spikes and thorns as to make their capture by anything but man seem nothing short of impossible, yet I have watched, with the same sensations as a man might view a big snake swallowing an ox whole, a shag swallow a large gurnard tail first—against the grain, as it were. This extraordinary and surely gratuitously painful feat took the shag just over half an hour of grotesque convulsion, and when the stunt was at last completed the bird had entirely changed its shape. From being a slim, graceful, snake-like creature with a neck like an ebony cane, it had become an amorphous and neck-less lump—its crop so gigantically distended as to force the head far back down the spine and flush with it—unable to rise or even to swim without danger of ridicule.

Mij himself caught a number of fish on his daily outings; and week by week, as his skill and speed grew, their size and variety increased. In the burn he learned to feel under stones for eels, reaching in with one paw and averted head; and I in turn learned to turn over the larger stones for him, so that after a time he would stand in front of some boulder too heavy for him to move, and chitter at me to come and lift it for him. Often, as I did this, an eel would streak out from it into deeper water and he would fire himself after it like a brown torpedo beneath the surface. Near the edge of the tide he would search out the perfectly camouflaged flounders until they shot off with a wake of rising sand-grains like smoke from an express train—and farther out in the bay he would kill an occasional sea trout; these he never brought ashore, but ate them treading water as he did so, while I thought a little wistfully of the Chinese who are said to employ trained otters to fish for them. Mij, I thought, with all his delightful camaraderies, would never offer me a fish; I was wrong, but when at last he did so it was not a sea trout but a flounder. One day he emerged from the sea on to the rock ledge where I was standing and slapped down in front of me a flounder a foot across. I took it that he had brought this for congratulation, for he would often bring his choicer catches for inspection before consuming them, so I said something encouraging and began to walk on. He hurried after me and slammed it down again with a wet smack at my feet. Even then I did not understand, assuming only that he wished to eat in company, but he just sat there looking up and chittering at me. I was in no hurry to take the gesture at its face value, for, as I have said, one of the most aggressive actions one can perform to a wild animal is to deprive it of its prey, but after perhaps half a minute of doubt, while Mij redoubled his invitation, I reached down slowly and cautiously for the fish, knowing that Mij would give me vocal warning if I had misinterpreted him. He watched me with the plainest approval while I picked it up and began a mime of eating it; then he plunged off the rock into the sea and sped away a fathom down in the clear water.

Watching Mij in a rough sea—and the equinoctial gales at Camusfeàrna produce very rough seas indeed—I was at first sick with apprehension, then awed and fascinated, for his powers seemed little less than miraculous. During the first of the gales, I remember, I tried to keep him to the rock pools and the more sheltered corners, but one day his pursuit of some unseen prey had taken him to the seaward side of a high dry reef at the very tide's edge. As the long undertow sucked outward he was in no more than an inch or two of marbled water with the rock at his back, crunching the small fish he had caught; then, some forty yards to seaward of him I saw a great snarling comber piling up higher and higher, surging in fifteen feet tall and as yet unbreaking. I yelled to Mij as the wave towered darkly towards him, but he went on eating and paid no heed to me. It curled over and broke just before it reached him; all those tons of water just smashed down and obliterated him, enveloping the whole rock behind in a booming tumult of sea. Somewhere under it I visualized Mij's smashed body swirling round the foot of the black rock. But as the sea drew back in a long hissing undertow I saw, incredulously, that nothing had changed; there was Mij still lying in the shallow marbled water, still eating his fish.

He rejoiced in the waves; he would hurl himself straight as an arrow right into the great roaring grey wall of an oncoming breaker and go clean through it as if it had neither weight nor momentum; he would swim far out to sea through wave after wave until the black dot of his head was lost among the distant white manes, and more than once I thought that some wild urge to seek new lands had seized him and that he would go on swimming west into the Sea of the Hebrides and that I should not see him again.

As the weeks went by his absences did grow longer, and I spent many anxious hours searching for him, though as yet he had never stayed away for a night. When I had drawn blank at the falls and at all his favourite pools in the burn or among the rock ledges by the sea, I would begin to worry and to roam more widely, calling his name all the while. His answering note of recognition was so like the call of some small dowdy bird that inhabits the trees by the waterside that my heart would leap a hundred times before I knew with certainty that I had heard his voice, and then my relief was so unbounded that I would allow him to dry me without protest.

The first time that I found him in distress was in the dark ravine above the waterfall. The waterfall divides, in some sense, the desert from the sown; the habitable world from the strange, beautiful, but inhospitable world of the dark gorge through which the burn flows above it. In summer, when the water is low, one may pick one's way precariously along the rock at the stream's edge, the almost sheer but wooded sides rising a hundred feet at either hand. Here it is always twilight, for the sun never reaches the bed of the stream, and in summer the sky's light comes down thin and diffused by a stipple of oak and birch leaves whose branches lean out far overhead. Here and there a fallen tree-trunk spans the narrow gorge, its surface worn smooth by the passage of the wildcats' feet. The air is cool, moist, and pungent with the smell of wild garlic and watery things such as ferns and mosses that grow in the damp and the dark. Sometimes the bed of the stream widens to deep pools whose rock flanks afford no foothold, and where it looks as though the black water must be bottomless.

Once Morag asked me, in an offhand way behind which I sensed a tentative probing, whether I felt at ease in that place. It was a question that held a tacit confession, and I replied frankly. I have never been at ease in it; it evokes in me an unpleasant sensation that I associate only with the unfurnished top floor of a certain house, a sensation which makes me want to glance constantly over my shoulder, as though, despite the physical impossibility, I were being followed. I catch myself trying to step silently from stone to stone, as though it were important to my safety that my presence should remain undetected. I should have been abashed to tell Morag of this had she not given me the lead, but she told me then that she had had a horror of the place ever since she was a child, and could offer no explanation.

To conform to the spirit of my confession the gorge ought, of course, to be shunned by bird and animal alike, but it has, in fact, more of both than one might expect. There are foxes' and badgers' and wildcats' dens in the treacherous, near-vertical walls of the ravine; the buzzards and hooded crows nest every year in the branches that lean out over the dark water; below them there are the dippers and grey wagtails (a crass ornithological misnomer for this canary-yellow creature), and, for some reason, an unusual number of wrens that skulk and twitter among the fern. Whatever makes the gorge an unpleasant place to some people does not extend its influence beyond human beings.

The deep pools spill in unbroken falls a few feet high, and after two hundred yards or so there is the second real waterfall, dropping fifty feet interrupted by a ledge pool half-way down. That is the upper limit of the 'haunting', though the physical details of the gorge above the second falls differ little from those of the stretch below it; then, a further hundred yards up the burn's course, the way is blocked by the tall cataract, eighty feet of foaming white water falling sheer.

Mij, certainly, found nothing distasteful in the reach where my ghosts walked, and he had early used his strength and resource to scale the Camusfeàrna waterfall and find out what lay beyond. Thereafter this inaccessible region had become his especial haunt, and one from which his extraction presented, even when he was not in difficulties, almost insuperable problems. The clamour of the falling water effectively drowned the calling human voice, and even if he did hear it there was little chance of the caller perceiving his faint, bird-like response. On this occasion there was more water in the burn than is usual in summer, and there had been, too, a recent landslide, temporarily destroying the only practicable access from above. I lowered myself into the ravine on a rope belayed to the trunk of a tree, and I was wet to the waist after the first few yards of the burn's bed. I called and called, but my voice was diminished and lost in the sound of rushing water, and the little mocking birds answered me with Mij's own note of greeting. At length one of these birds, it seemed, called so repeatedly and insistently as to germinate in me a seed of doubt, but the sound came from far above me, and I was looking for Mij in the floor of the burn. Then I saw him; high up on the cliff, occupying so small a ledge that he could not even turn to make his way back, and with a fifty-foot sheer drop below him; he was looking at me, and, according to his lights, yelling his head off. I had to make a long detour to get above him with the rope and all the while I was terrified that the sight of me would have spurred him to some effort that would bring tragedy; terrified, too, that I myself might dislodge him as I tried to lift him from his eyrie. Then I found that the trees at the cliff-top were all rotten, and I had to make the rope fast to a stump on the hill above, a stump that grew in soft peat and that gave out from its roots an ominous squelching sound when I tugged hard on it. I went down that rock with the rope knotted round my waist and the feeling that Mij would probably survive somehow, but that I should most certainly die. He tried to stand on his hind legs when he saw me coming down above him, and more than once I thought he had gone. I had put the loop of his lead through the rope at my waist, and I clipped the other end to his harness as soon as my arm could reach him, but the harnesses, with their constant immersion, never lasted long, and I trusted this one about as much as I trusted the stump to which my rope was tied. I went up the rope with Mij dangling and bumping at my side like a cow being loaded on to a ship by crane, and in my mind's eye were two jostling, urgent images—the slow, sucking emergence of the tree roots above me, and the gradual parting of the rivets that held Mij's harness together. All in all it was one of the nastiest five minutes of my life; and when I reached the top the roots of the stump were indeed showing—it took just one tug with all my strength to pull them clean out.

But the harness had held, though, mercifully, it broke the next time it was put to strain. Mij had been missing, that day in the ravine, for nine hours, and had perhaps passed most of them on that ledge, for he was ravenously hungry, and ate until I thought he must choke.

There were other absences, other hours of anxiety and search, but one in particular stands out in my mind, for it was the first time that he had been away for a whole night, the first time that I despaired of him. I had left him in the early morning at the burn side eating his eels, and began to be uneasy when he had not returned by mid-afternoon. I had been working hard at my book; it was one of those rare days of authorship when everything seemed to go right; the words flowed unbidden from my pen, and the time had passed unheeded, so that it was a shock to realize that I had been writing for some six hours. I went out and called for Mij down the burn and along the beach, and when I did not find him I went again to the ravine above the falls. But there was no trace of him anywhere, though I explored the whole dark length of it right to the high falls, which I knew that even Mij could not pass. Just how short a distance my voice carried I realized when, above the second falls, I came upon two wildcat kittens at play on the steep bank; they saw me and were gone in a flash, but they had never heard my voice above the sound of the water. I left the burn then and went out to the nearer islands; it was low tide, and there were exposed stretches and bars of soft white sand. Here I found otter footprints leading towards the lighthouse island, but I could not be certain that they were Mij's. Later that summer his claws became worn so that his pad-marks no longer showed the nails, but at that stage I was still unsure of distinguishing his tracks from those of a wild otter, unless the imprints were very precise. All that evening I searched and called, and when dusk came and he still did not return I began to despair, for his domestic life had led him to strictly diurnal habits, and by sundown he was always asleep in front of the fire.

It was a cloudy night with a freshening wind and a big moon that swam muzzily through black rags of vapour. By eleven o'clock it was blowing strong to gale from the south, and on the windward side of the islands there was a heavy sea beginning to pile up; enough, I thought, for him to lose his bearings if he were trying to make his way homeward through it. I put a light in each window of the house, left the doors open, and dozed fitfully in front of the kitchen fire. By three o'clock in the morning there was the first faint paling of dawn, and I went out to get the boat, for by now I had somehow convinced myself that Mij was on the lighthouse island. That little cockleshell was in difficulties from the moment I launched her; I had open water and a beam sea to cross before I could reach the lee of the islands, and she was taking a slosh of water over her gunwale all the way. If I shipped oars to bale I made so much leeway that I was nearly ashore again before I had done, and after half an hour I was both wet and scared. The bigger islands gave some shelter from the south wind, but in the passages between them the north-running sea was about as much as the little boat would stand, and over the many rocks and skerries the water was foaming white and wicked-looking in the half light. A moment to bale and I would have been swept on to these black cusps and molars; the boat would have been crunched on them like a squashed matchbox, and I, who cannot swim a stroke, would have been feeding the lobsters. To complete my discomfort, I met a Killer whale. In order to keep clear of the reefs I had rowed well north of the small islands that lie to landward of the lighthouse; the water was calmer here, and I did not have to fight to keep the nose of the boat into the waves. The Killer broke the surface no more than twenty yards to the north of me, a big bull whose sabre fin seemed to tower a man's height out of the water; and, probably by chance, he turned straight for me. My nerves were strung and tensed, and I was in no frame of mind to assess the true likelihood of danger; I swung and rowed for the nearest island as though man were a Killer's only prey. I grounded on a reef a hundred yards from the tern island, and I was not going to wait for the tide to lift me. Slithering and floundering in thigh-deep water over a rock ledge I struggled until I had lifted the flat keel clear of the tooth on which it had grated; the Killer, possibly intent upon his own business and with no thought for me, cruised round a stone's throw away. I reached the tern island, and the birds rose screaming around me in a dancing canopy of ghostly wings, and I sat down on the rock in the dim windy dawn and felt as desolate as an abandoned child.

The lighthouse island was smothered in its jungle-growth of summer briars that grip the clothing with octopus arms and leave trails of blood-drops across hands and face; on it I felt like a dream walker who never moves, and my calling voice was swept away northwards on gusts of cold, wet wind. I got back to the house at nine in the morning, with a dead-weight boat more than half full of water and a sick emptiness in my mind and body. By now part of me was sure that Mij too had met the Killer, and that he was at this moment half digested in the whale's belly.

All that day until four o'clock in the afternoon I wandered and called, and with every hour grew the realization of how much that strange animal companion had come to signify to me. I resented it, resented my dependence upon this subhuman presence and companionship, resented the void that his absence was going to leave at Camusfeàrna. It was in this mood, one of reassertion of human independence, that about five in the evening I began to remove the remaining evidence of his past existence. I had taken from beneath the kitchen table his drinking bowl, had returned for the half-full bowl of rice and egg, had carried this to the scullery, what the Scots call the back kitchen, and was about to empty it into the slop pail, when I thought I heard Mij's voice from the kitchen behind me. I was, however, very tired, and distrustful of my own reactions; what I thought I had heard was the harshly whispered 'Hah?' with which he was accustomed to interrogate a seemingly empty room. The impression was strong enough for me to set down the bowl and hurry back into the kitchen. There was nothing there. I walked to the door and called his name, but all was as it had been before. I was on my way back to the scullery when I stopped dead. There on the kitchen floor, where I had been about to step, was a large, wet footprint. I looked at it, and I thought: I am very tired and very overwrought; and I went down on my hands and knees to inspect it. It was certainly wet, and it smelled of otter. I was still in a quadrupedal attitude when from the doorway behind me I heard the sound again, this time past mistaking—'Hah?' Then Mij was all over me, drenched and wildly demonstrative, squeaking, bouncing round me like an excitable puppy, clambering on my shoulders, squirming on his back, leaping, dancing. I had been reassuring myself and him for some minutes before I realized that his harness was burst apart, and that for many hours, perhaps a day or more, he must have been caught like Absalom, struggling, desperate, waiting for a rescue that never came.

I am aware that this scene of reunion, and the hours that for me had preceded it, must appear to many a reader little short of nauseous. I might write of it and subsequent events with a wry dishonesty, a negation of my feeling for that creature, which might disarm criticism, might forestall the accusation of sentimentality and slushiness to which I now lay myself open. There is, however, a certain obligation of honesty upon a writer, without which his words are worthless, and beyond that my feeling for animals that I adopt would, despite any dissimulation that I might essay, reveal itself as intense, even crucial. I knew by that time that Mij meant more to me than most human beings of my acquaintance, that I should miss his physical presence more than theirs, and I was not ashamed of it. In the penultimate analysis, perhaps, I knew that Mij trusted me more utterly than did any of my own kind, and so supplied a need that we are slow to admit.

When I missed Mij from his accustomed haunts I would go first to the waterfall, for there he would spend long hours alone, chasing the one big trout that lived in the big pool below the falls, catching elvers, or playing with some floating object that had been washed down. Sometimes he would set out from the house carrying a ping-pong ball, purposeful and self engrossed, and he would still be at the waterfall with it an hour later, pulling it under water and letting it shoot up again, rearing up and pouncing on it, playing his own form of water polo, with a goal at which the human onlooker could but guess. Once, I remember, I went to look for him there and at first could not find him; then my attention was caught by something red in the black water at the edge of the foam, and I saw that Mij was floating on his back, apparently fast asleep, with a bunch of scarlet rowan berries clasped to his chest with one arm. Such bright objects as these he would often pick up on his walks, and carry them with him until some rival attraction supplanted them. I never performed any tests to define his degree of colour vision, but whether by chance or selection his preferred playthings were often of garish hue.

I was watching him at the waterfall one day, trying to take photographs of him as he frolicked with his ping-pong ball in the deep pool, when I lost my footing on the sloping rock and found myself in beside him, camera and all. I had just started back for the house to change my clothes when I heard voices. A dry-stone wall runs between the waterfall and the house, and when I reached this with Mij at my heels I saw a figure approaching me whom I recognized with difficulty as the literary editress of the *New Statesman*; with difficulty, because her clothes were far from conventional, and I had not previously seen her away from city surroundings. We exchanged greetings over the wall, and began to talk. Mij climbed on to the wall top beside me and watched.

Now Mij had an especial vice that I have not yet mentioned; a vice that I had been unable to cure, partly, anyway, because I did not understand its cause or motivation. To put it bluntly, he bit the lobes of people's ears—not, certainly, in anger nor in spite; not, apparently, as a conscious act of aggression or ill-will, but simply because he liked doing so. He collected them, so to speak, not as David collected the foreskins of the Philistines, in enmity, but as an amiable hobby. He just nipped through them like an efficient ear-piercer, and apparently felt the better for it. It was now so long since he had met strangers and had the opportunity to add an ear to his list that I had momentarily forgotten this deplorable proclivity. My visitor leaned an arm on the wall as she talked, with her head a mere foot from Mij's, and Mij reached out, without comment, and pierced the lobe of her left ear with surgical precision.

It was her finest hour. I had seen many lobes pierced by Mij; I was a connoisseur of reaction to the situation, ranging from the faint shriek, through gabbling reassurance, to the ominous flushed silence: I thought I knew them all, but I was wrong. Not by the smallest interruption in her flow of speech, not by so much as a hint of an indrawn breath did she betray that she had perceived the incident; only her eyes, as she continued her sentence, assumed an expression of unbelieving outrage entirely at variance with her words.

One of the few people who escaped this hall-mark, as it were, of Mij's acquaintance, was Morag. I myself had had both ears pierced early in my association with my namesake, and now enjoyed immunity. To only two other people did he extend the tempestuous affection that he accorded to me, to Morag and to Kathleen Raine; but though the degree of demonstrative love to each of us did not greatly differ it was quite unlike in kind—with each, that is to say, he formed an entirely different relationship. With Kathleen, whose mere proximity would send him into ecstasies, he was rough and rumbustious, fiercely possessive, and he took advantage of her whenever and however he could; she in turn found some strange community with him, and was prepared to put up uncomplainingly with his most exuberant horse play. With Morag he was gentler, less bullying, in his love, and with me more deferential, more responsive to the suggestion of command. But it remained around us three that his orb revolved when he was not away in his own imponderable world of wave and water, of dim green depths and tide-swayed fronds of the sea-tangle; we were his Trinity, and he behaved towards us much as Mediterranean people do towards theirs, with a mixture of trust and abuse, passion and irritation. In turn each of us in our own way depended, as gods do, upon his worship; I, perhaps, most of all, because he belonged to the only race of living creature that was ever likely to bear my name.

10

I RETURNED to London with Mij in the autumn, and with his usual good humour he adjusted himself quickly to the absence of his beloved burn and foreshore. During the car journey from Camusfeàrna to Inverness he seemed, in a long deep sleep, to shed his wild nature and to awake metamorphosed as a domestic animal. In the station hotel he lay beside my chair while I had tea, and when a waitress brought him a saucer of milk he lapped it as delicately as any drawing-room cat, spilling never a drop. He entered his first-class sleeper as one long used to travel, and at the studio next morning he seemed actively pleased to be among his old surroundings. He settled quickly, too, into his earlier routine; eels in the bath; walks round the grubby London streets; even, not without trepidation on my part, an afternoon's shopping in Harrods. By one local shop he was allowed to make his own selection before purchase; he had, as I have mentioned, a passion for rubber toys, more especially such as would squeak or rattle when manipulated. Near by to my flat was a shop devoted entirely to such oddities; india-rubber fruit and buns, explosive cigars, apparently full glasses from which no drop of liquid could escape, even papier mâché imitations of dog and cat excrement— the whole practical joker's compendium. Here I was hesitating one day between a chocolate éclair that whistled and an india-rubber mackerel that wheezed when the assistant said, 'Why not let him make his own choice, sir?' and placed both on the floor. Mij plumped for the éclair, to the assistant's surprise, and there-after Mij chose his own toys and himself bore them home in triumph. It was a very realistic éclair, and as we passed the door of the pub on the corner a figure emerged swaying slightly, focused Mij, and stood riveted. 'Good God!' he said, quite quietly, and behind him a voice shouted, 'You've got 'em again, Bill—you've got 'em again!'

Mij seemed in those days to possess a quality of indestructibility, an imperviousness to physical hurt, that was little short of miraculous. He succeeded, despite all my precautions, in falling from the gallery to the parquet floor below, but he might, for all the notice he took of the incident, have fallen upon a feather bed; his head was caught, without protest, in a slamming door; and, finally, he chewed a razor blade into fragments. I had been out for the evening, and had left him the premises beyond the kitchen, the bathroom, that is to say, with a full bath, and beyond it the box-room where he had a tattered armchair of his own and an electric fire that shone down upon it from the wall. When I came in I opened the bathroom door and called him, but there was no response. I went in and saw that the bath was empty of water; at the bottom of it my safety razor was in two pieces, lying among splintered pieces of the blade. It did not at that instant strike me that the total absence of blood indicated, however improbably, an intact otter; I went through into the box-room expecting to find a corpse in the chair beneath the warm glow of the fire. But there among the cushions he was squirming with self-satisfaction, as though conscious of having carried out a difficult task with initiative and acumen, and there was not, as far as I could discover, so much as a scratch on him.

I cannot now remember whether, when I had been in Iraq, I had ever seriously considered what was to be done with an otter during such times as I was unable to look after him myself; when, for example, I was again abroad, or even when I wanted to be away from my own premises for a day or two. Perhaps I had thought that at any rate in the latter case he could accompany me, for I had not yet learned that an otter is not at its best as a guest in a strange house—or rather that the house would be very strange indeed at the end of the visit. Mij was content to be alone for four or five hours, but for no longer unless those hours began in the evening, and now I found my activities so hamstrung by this dependence that I was forced to take the problem seriously.

In November I had to be away from London for three days, to lecture in the Midlands, and this was Mij's first and only imprisonment away from the people and surroundings that he knew. I arranged for him to be boarded for those three days at the zoo sanatorium, and took him up to Regent's Park in a taxi. Once inside the gardens he plodded sturdily ahead at the end of his lead, and for all his reaction the teeming animal voices and smells around him might not have existed. Only when he passed by the aviaries containing the great birds of prey did he cower and tug his lead the other way; a memory, perhaps, of his native marshes where, winter long, the eagles wheel above the wastes of water, and where they must be the otter's only natural enemy; or perhaps an inborn instinct that his race's foes came from the skies. I left him in a grim cage whose last occupant had been a sick wart-hog, and when the door was closed on him and he found himself alone his wails went to my heart. I could hear him long after I had closed the gate of the sanatorium yard.

On the evening of the next day I telephoned from the north to enquire if he had settled down. Too much, I was told; in fact he had insulated himself from the world by the same deep coma into which he had sunk when shut into a box on the air journey. He had refused all food, and after digging at the iron and cement that enclosed him until his feet bled he had curled up in my sheep-skin coat and refused to be roused. I was advised to come back for him as soon as possible; not rarely pet animals in such surroundings would pass almost imperceptibly from such a coma into death.

I left for London very early the next morning, but there was a dense white fog which slowed me to a bicycle's speed for the first hundred miles. Then it furled up suddenly to reveal a bare blue sky and bright autumn sunshine. My car was a ferocious vehicle, converted from a single-seater Grand Prix racing car, and in her distant prime speeds in excess of 160 m.p.h. had been claimed for her, but at this moment I was running-in a set of new pistons that she seemed to require about as often as more modest

143

conveyances need refilling with petrol. With that last hundred miles the running-in distance was, on the milometer, completed, but in my anxiety to reach London and my pining otter I left out of account that they had been covered so slowly as to be valueless for the purpose. I came out on to the long straight north of Grantham, and unfortunately there was not another car in sight to slow me down. I had been driving at about 90 m.p.h.; now, I thought, I would go very much faster, and, for a short time, I did. The supercharger screamed, dial needles moved with incredible rapidity towards red zones; I had a glimpse of the speedometer hovering at 145 m.p.h., and I was still accelerating briskly. Then there was a rending sound, the cockpit filled with a great puff of blue smoke, and in the mirror I saw a thin black trail of oil stretching away behind me. I came to rest opposite to a farmhouse, and all I could think of was whether a train could get me to London before the staff of the zoo sanatorium went off duty in the evening. The farm had a telephone; the only possible train left Grantham in thirty-eight minutes, and I caught it as it was moving out of the station.

Back at the zoo sanatorium, I could not at first even see Mij in his cage. There were a lot of dead fish lying about untouched, and a big basin the size of a hip bath had been slopped about so that there was water everywhere; the sheepskin jacket was lying in a huddle in the middle of this, and there was no movement anywhere. I came in through the steel-barred door and called his name, but nothing stirred. I put my hand into the jacket and I felt him warm and breathing, as far into the arm hole as he could push himself. Only when I thrust my hand in beside him until I could touch his face did he begin to awaken, with a slow, dazed air as if he were emerging from a trance; then suddenly he was out and leaping in a frenzy of joy, clambering over me and inside my coat, and rushing round and round that barren cage until he threw himself down panting in front of me.

In those two days he had taken on the sour small-cat-house odour of stale urine and dejection and indignity that is the hall-mark of the captive; he had lost his self respect and fouled his own bed, so that his usually sweet-smelling fur stank like an ill-kept ferret. It was not an experiment that I ever repeated, but his boarding was clearly a problem to which I had to find a solution.

He paid one more visit to the zoo, but this time not as a captive. I had for long wanted to have a clear, eye-level view of his performance under-water, and to this end I was allowed by the Zoological Society to erect in the back premises of the Aquarium a large glass tank that I had hired for the day. Had I known that there was never to be another opportunity I would have arranged for a cinema camera, but as things were I asked Michael Ayrton to come and make drawings of him. With the tank I was provided with a number of goldfish for Mij to catch and consume; I could have wished that there had been something of more feral appearance, something associated less in the mind's eye with the parlour and the aspidistra and the loving care of an old maid, or with the cosy, unpredatory world of the nursery, where only in fiction was nature permitted to be red in tooth and claw. Mij, however, was untroubled by any such connotations, and set about their destruction with a zeal and a display of virtuosity for which even my long hours of watching him from above had left me unprepared. His speed was bewildering, his grace breath-taking; he was boneless, mercurial, sinuous, wonderful. I thought of a trapeze artist, of a ballet dancer, of a bird or an aircraft in aerobatics, but in all these I was comparing him to lesser grandeurs; he was an otter in his own element, and he was the most beautiful thing in nature that I had ever seen.

As with his toys, he was not content to be in possession of only one fish at a time; having captured the first he would tuck it under one arm, and, apparently utterly unhandicapped by this awkward parcel, would swoop, sometimes 'looping the loop' as he did so, upon another; at one moment he had fish under both arms and a third in his mouth. At the conclusion of this display, which had cost me in hire charges some ten shillings a minute, I felt that I had seldom been so richly rewarded for financial outlay on visual experience, and I determined that I must have a glass tank of my own for him in London.

I began my own search for emancipation by inserting an advertisement in *Country Life*, the *Field*, and *The Times*, requesting in gist a temporary home for Mij where he could be left for anything from days to months as necessity demanded. Altogether I received some forty replies to this somewhat egregious demand, and conscientiously followed up every one of them, but one by one the prospective guardians were weighed and found wanting. Few of them had any idea of what they would be taking on; fewer still had premises in any way suitable; some turned out to be schoolchildren applying without their parents' knowledge. At the end of two months I was no further on than on the day I had drafted the advertisement.

Then I began to interview retired zoo keepers, but a few weeks of this convinced me that a retired zoo keeper has an implacable intention to remain retired. Meanwhile the book that I had been writing was finished, and I should in the normal course of events have begun again to travel. It seemed an impasse. Though I found a temporary solution—to return to Camusfeàrna in the spring and there to write a book about Mij—these were clearly no more than delaying tactics, and with friends in the zoological world I left an urgent plea to find me, by hook or by crook, a whole-time otter-keeper. But by the time he was found and engaged, Mij was dead.

What little there remains to tell of his story I shall write quickly, for anyone who in reading it has shared a little of my pleasure in his life must share, too, a little of my unhappiness at his death.

I had arranged to go to Camusfeàrna to spend the spring and summer alone in his company, and there to write the book about him that I had projected. I was to leave London early in April, but I needed a fortnight's freedom from his incessant demands upon my time, and I arranged that he should precede me to Scotland in the charge of a friend. I packed his 'suitcase', a wicker basket whose essential contents seemed ever to become more and more elaborate—spare harnesses, leads, tins of unpolished rice, cod-liver oil, toys partially disintegrated but long favoured, and I travelled with him in the hired car from my flat to Euston station. It was a big Humber, with a broad ledge between the top of the back seat and the rear window; here, I recall with a vividness that is still in some sense painful, he sprawled upon his back and rolled my fountain pen to and fro between his forepaws, or held it clasped with one of them against his broad, glossy belly. I called my companion's attention to the rich sheen of his coat reflecting the neon lights. He was in his most domesticated mood.

At the station he tugged purposefully at the lead all the way up the astonished platform to the sleeper, where he made straight for the wash basin and accommodated his plastic body to the curves. His left hand reached up and fumbled vaguely with the tap. That was the last I ever saw of him.

During the next ten days I received letters telling me of Mij's delight in his renewed freedom, of the fish that he had caught in the river and in the sea; of how he would come in dog-tired and curl up before the fire; of anxious hours of absence; of how it had been decided at last that he would be safer without his harness, which, despite the care and experiment that had gone to its design, might still catch upon some under-water snag and drown him.

On 16th April I had packed my own luggage, and was to be at Camusfeàrna myself the following afternoon, when I received a telephone call from the estate agent of the property to which Camusfeàrna belonged. It was rumoured, he told me, that an otter had been killed at the village four miles north of Camusfeàrna, and Mij was missing. There was, however, a discrepancy; the otter that had been killed was said to have been so mangy and scabby that the killer had not thought it worth while to preserve the skin. There was no detailed information.

Nor was there to be any yet; no tidy end, no body to identify, no palliative burial at the foot of the rowan tree; no human kindness that would spare to those who had been fond of him the day-long search, the door standing open all through the night.

I arrived at the village the following afternoon. I had heard conflicting tales at the railhead station, on the launch that took me to the village, at the village pier. Some said that a very old wild otter had been killed, but that Mij was already safely returned, others that he had been seen in a village miles to the south of

Camusfeàrna. I did not believe them; I knew that Mij was dead, but I was driven by a compulsive desire to know by whom and how he had been killed.

A roadman, I was told in the village, had been driving his lorry past the church when he had seen an otter on the road where it bordered the sea, and had killed it. The skin was partly hairless and he had not kept it.

I found out where this man lived, and drove some four miles inland to see his family. I arrived furtively, for I expected to find Mij's pelt nailed out to dry somewhere in the environs of the house—a thing I should not be allowed to see if I made my enquiry first. For me it would have felt like finding the skin of a human friend, but I had to know.

The family denied all knowledge of it. The skin, they said, had been so mangy that the killer, Big Angus, had thrown it away before reaching home. No, they didn't know where. Big Angus was not back yet—he would come riding on the pillion of a motor-cycle; if I was to wait in the village I might see him.

I waited. The motor-cycle came at last. Yes, it was true that he had killed an otter yesterday, but it was also true that the skin was half bald, and he had not thought it worth keeping. He was soft-spoken and ingenuous.

I asked him to show me where it had happened. I walked back with him some two hundred yards to a sharp bend where a little churchyard lay between the road and the sea. He had come round the corner with his lorry, and the otter had been there, just above the road, in the ditch. He had stopped his lorry.

I could see it desperately plainly. 'How did you kill him?' I asked. 'With a stick?' 'No, Major,' he said, 'I had a pick-head in the back of the lorry.' He thought that a wild otter would wait in the road while he went to fetch the instrument of its death. He stuck to his story; by his account the otter he had killed could not have been mine. 'He was very old and skinny,' he said again and again. 'I threw the carcase in the river, and I don't remember where.' He had been well briefed and well rehearsed, as I learned much later, when he had gone in panic to seek advice. Brave murderer; for his lies and deceit I could have killed him then as

In the garden at Monreith

Mijbil soon after his arrival in England

Mijbil drying himself in the sand

Playing on the floor of the studio

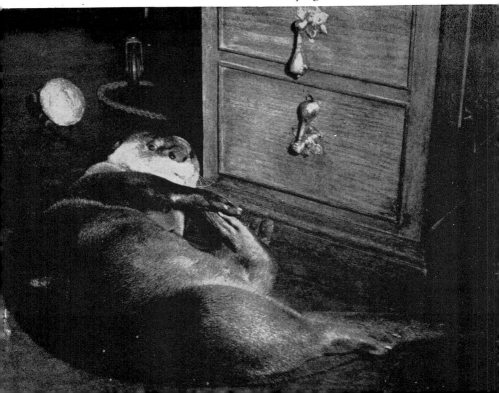

At the top of his toboganning slide at Camusfeàrna

'An established selection of toys'

A lost marble

Asleep before the gas fire in London.

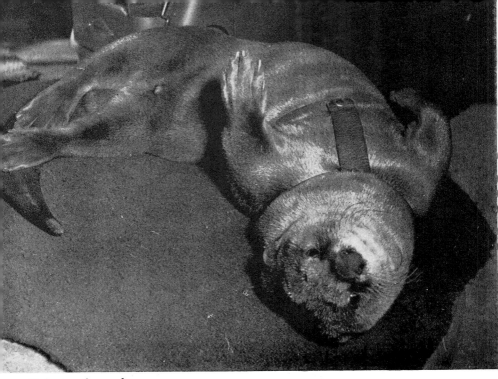

Relaxing from play

An eye on the photographer

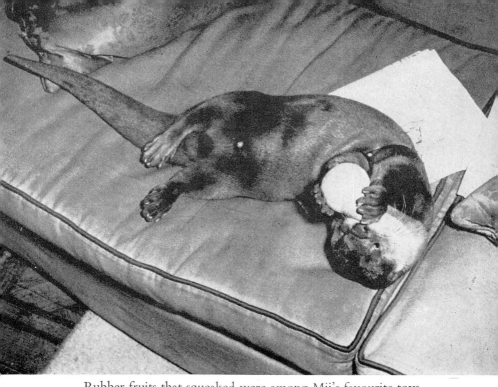

Rubber fruits that squeaked were among Mij's favourite toys

Lutrogale perspicillata maxwelli

instinctively and with as little forethought as he had killed the creature I had brought so many thousands of miles, killed him quickly and treacherously, when he was expecting it no more than Mij had, so that the punishment would fit the crime.

Instead, I appealed foolishly to the quality he lacked; I pleaded with him to tell me; I tried to make him understand what it would be like for me to remain at Camusfeàrna waiting day after day for the return that I did not believe possible. He did not give way an inch.

I learned later, from someone else with more humanity.

'I felt I couldn't sit by and see you deceived,' he said. 'It's just not a decent action in a man, and that's the truth. I saw the body of the beast on the lorry when it stopped in the village, and there wasn't a hair out of place on the whole skin—except the head, which was all bashed in. If he didn't know fine it was yours he knew then, because I told him; "You want to get your head seen to," I said, "if you think that's a wild otter, or if you think a wild one would wait for you to kill it in broad daylight." It's just a pack of lies he's telling you, and I couldn't think of you looking and calling for your pet up and down the burn and by the tide every day, and him dead all the while.'

I got the story little by little. Mij had been wandering widely for some days past, and though he had always returned at night he must have covered great distances, for he had turned up one day at a hamlet some eight miles south by sea. There he had been recognized and gone unmolested; the next day he had journeyed north up the coast to the village where he was killed. Earlier in the day he had been recognized there too; a man who saw an otter in his hen run had fetched his gun before he was struck by the otter's indifference to the chickens, and made the right deduction. Mij had been on his way home when he had met Big Angus, and he had never been taught to fear or distrust any human being. I hope he was killed quickly, but I wish he had had one chance to use his teeth on his killer.

He had been with me for a year and a day on the night he had left London.

11

I MISSED Mij desperately, so much that it was a year before I could bring myself to go to Camusfeàrna again. I mourned for my fallen sparrow; he had filled that landscape so completely, had made so much his own every yard of the ring of bright water I loved, that it seemed, after he had gone from it, hollow and insufficient; for the first time all the familiar things in which I had taken joy appeared as a stage backcloth against which no player moved. I did not stay there after I knew that he was dead; instead, I returned at once to Sicily, and resumed a work that had by now been long interrupted. As the slow summer months passed under that scorching sun the year during which I had had an otter for a companion, and even Camusfeàrna itself, seemed at times like a dream. I could not deny to myself how much I had been affected by the death of one wild animal, but some part of me stood aside and questioned the validity, the morality, perhaps, of such an attitude in face of the human misery surrounding me. Like my occupancy of the Isle of Soay, that year now appeared to me episodic, sharply defined at beginning and end, and without possible extension; but, as in that other instance, I was wrong.

I came back from Sicily in the autumn, and moved house to Chelsea, partly, I must confess, because I found the elaboration of otter-proofing devices that now composed my premises to be too constant and nagging a reminder of my failure to keep alive an animal to which I had given so much attention. But I had grown accustomed to the continual proximity of an animal, and when one day in Harrods I found a Ring-tailed Lemur, lately the property of Cyril Connolly, not even the price of seventy-five pounds could discourage me from my folly. Kiko, as she was called, came to live in my new flat. Kiko was an exceedingly beautiful animal rather larger than a very large cat, an *haute couture* creation in soft blue-grey fur, with a foxy black-and-white face, a great bushy tail of alternating black and white rings, golden eyes, monkey hands with straight needle-pointed claws, and habits that were both insanitary and obscene. For the greater part of the time she remained almost perpetually on heat; what was noticeable, however, was not so much the heat as the humidity. For the rest, she had some deep-seated psychosis that made her about as suitable a pet as a wild-caught leopard. For nine hundred and ninety-nine minutes out of every thousand she was as loving and gentle as any child might wish; for that remaining minute she was a killer, attacking without warning or *casus belli*, and always from behind. Her technique of inflicting grievous bodily harm was to spring from some high bookcase to one's shoulder—she could leap twenty feet without apparent effort—and claw for the eyes with the rending pins on her fingers. Whatever the early traumatic experience responsible for this hideous treachery, it was, I deduce, concerned in some way with windows, for each of her three attacks was launched when I was standing at a window, and, for one purpose or another, touching it; at the moment of the third and final outrage I was talking through the window to someone on the pavement outside.

I think I was fortunate not to have been killed by Kiko, for I ignored the danger signs for far too long. I chose to regard my slit eyelid as an accident, thinking that she had lost her balance and clawed without intent. The next time I defended my eyes with my hands, and as a result bear scars that I shall never lose, for her teeth were slashing instruments with razor-sharp edges. I excused this on the ground that she had interpreted my movement as a gesture of aggression. The next time I used my arms rather than my hands to cover my eyes, and Kiko lost balance and fell to the floor. She seemed to me to be making angry feints at my legs, but I was unaware of any actual contact before I noticed, with something very like panic, that I was standing in a large and rapidly-widening puddle of blood. I knew that nothing but an artery could have produced that astonishing volume; I got out of the room somehow, and made for the bathroom, leaving behind me a trail of blood that appeared appropriate to a slaughterhouse. There I found that my tibial artery was sticking out of my calf like a black cigarette end, and spouting blood to a distance of more than a foot. I soaked a handkerchief and tried to apply a tourniquet, but my knowledge had deserted me; I could not remember the pressure point. At the end of several minutes trying here and there I estimated that I had by now lost something like two pints of blood, and I wasted several more seconds trying to calculate how soon I should lose consciousness, for I was already beginning to feel weak and shaky. I made out that at the present rate of loss I had a little over five minutes, and I was searching wildly for some thread to tie the artery when I suddenly had a perfect mental picture of a huge wall chart showing the venous system in red and the arterial in blue. The tibial artery, of course, only surfaced at the groin. I got the tourniquet on and a cigarette lit and began to think about Kiko. The psychoanalysis of a lemur, I realized, would present insuperable problems. She now shares spacious accommodation with three other ring-tailed lemurs in the Chester Zoo. She is still mine, and once I hoped that she would breed and I might rear her offspring well sheltered from trauma, but now I feel that lemurs, sharing as they do a common ancestor with man, might require as careful choosing as do human friends.

After Kiko came a Bush Baby, who, apart from the wholly misleading blood-curdling shriek with which he would nightly challenge the sleeping jungle of Chelsea, turned out to be a really crashing bore; his hobbies, moreover, were solitary and embarrassing. Later, after he had moved on to less exacting ownership than mine, I was offered another with the curious but most appropriate name of Hitchcock; though he proved, in fact, to have been christened by the surname of his owners, it was a reminder, and I declined.

I did not experiment with any other animals; none of these creatures, had, anyway, the least affinity with Camusfeàrna. I acquired, instead, a baker's dozen of small, brilliant tropical birds, who flew at liberty about my sitting-room; they proved to be both less insanitary and less dangerous than Kiko.

If Camusfeàrna had lacked one obvious element of conventional romance it was buried treasure, not symbolic treasure,
but the hard practical glitter of coins in the peat. Now, but alas
during my year of absence, the lily was thus gilded. Two forestry
workers, digging ditches on the hill-side above the house, came
upon a small hoard of coins, hidden or dropped, together with
fragments of hide in which they had been once contained. They
were for the most part coins of the 16th century, of Mary Tudor,
Philip and Mary, Elizabeth, and James I, and one, the largest of
them all, a dollar piece of Frederick Ulric Duke of Brunswick and
Luneburg; the savings, probably of some soldier of fortune, a
mercenary who, like many Highlanders of old, had sold his
sword and his courage to the service of foreign commanders. The
cache, if cache it was rather than a purse hurriedly hidden when
the enemy was already in sight, must have been a secret kept to
himself; and whether he died fighting in some far-off land or in
the bitter, vicious skirmishes of clan warfare, his treasure had
thereafter remained undisturbed for more than three centuries.

In the early spring of the following year I made up my mind to
go back to Camusfeàrna. There, with the cold, bright March
weather shining on the landscape that had long become my real
home, I found myself assailed again by echoes of the emptiness
that I had experienced when Mij was killed; dimly at first, and
then clear and undisguised, came the thought that the place was
incomplete without an otter, that Mij must have a successor; that,
in fact, there must always be an otter at Camusfeàrna for as long
as I occupied the house.

Having at last made up my mind, I turned all my attention to
this end. With vivid recollection of my slavery to Mij's exigence,
I wrote first to the zoological friends who had offered to find an
otter-keeper for me, and then began a systematic examination of
all the holts I knew up and down the coast from Camusfeàrna.
One of the chain of islands leading out from the bay is called
Otter Island, and on it is a tumbled cairn of big boulders forming
a system of low caves much used by otters; in an earlier year,
before I had become as it were otter-conscious, there had been a
litter of cubs there. But now, though several of the inner chambers

had been well ordered and lined with fresh bedding, there was no sign of young, and the public lavatory was little used. There is a lavatory at every otter holt, and the excrement (which is known as 'spraint', and has no offensive odour, being composed almost entirely of crunched fish bones, or, in the case of shore-living otters, of fragments of crab carapace) often forms a high pyramidal pile; on the very top of one such I remember seeing, in that year when the cubs were on Otter Island, a tiny caterpillar of spraint whose deposition must have been an acrobatic feat for the tottering cub.

One by one I visited all the holts of which I knew, but there seemed no otters breeding in the Camusfeàrna area. I did not despair of acquiring a cub locally, for otters have no 'breeding season', and cubs have been found in every month of the year, but as a second string I wrote to Robert Angorly in Basra, and asked if he could arrange with the Marsh Arabs to get me another of Mij's species.

In response to Angorly's request the Marsh Arabs brought in a succession of cubs, three of which were *Lutrogale perspicillata maxwelli*, but each in turn died within a few days of arrival. This he at last put down to the fact that for days before arrival they had been tended by ungentle and inexpert hands; now he said flatly that he would accept no cub that had been more than twelve hours captive. As a result, the next cub lived, and in late June he wrote to tell me that I could arrange her transport to England when I liked. She was not, he said, a Maxwell's Otter, but he personally believed her to belong to yet another undiscovered race. She lived in the house, and was as playful and friendly as any dog.

With this apparent certainty of a successor to Mij, I began to make elaborate preparations, for I was anxious to make the fullest use of my hard-earned experience. My early enquiries for an otter-keeper had at last borne fruit, and now I was able to engage Jimmy Watt, a boy leaving school, who, though without first-hand knowledge of otters, had a profound natural feeling for animals and a desire to work with them. In London I had a large glass tank erected in the garden.

I had arranged for the otter to be flown from Basra to London on Thursday, 10th July, but the glazing of this tank was still uncompleted on the preceding Monday, and I telegraphed to Angorly asking him to postpone dispatch until the same flight on Tuesday the 15th.

On Monday, 14th July, revolution swept Iraq, and on that Tuesday they were playing football with the Crown Prince's head in the streets of Baghdad. Of Robert Angorly, who by nature of his office as chief game warden numbered as one of the tyrant's personal entourage, I have heard no word since.

One incident stands out from that golden, Mediterranean summer at Camusfeàrna, a summer spoiled only by my own small vacuum of frustration, my little foxes that spoiled the vines and robbed my loved landscape of its full stimulus.

This was a spectacle of such magnificence and magnitude that it should, perhaps, have quelled in me an obsession as freakish as the desire for the companionship of a particular species of wild animal. Often before I had seen the Northern Lights, the Aurora Borealis, flicker and tremble across the silent night sky above the mountains, but never, until that night, had I understood their fearful majesty, or the sense of utter negation that they could bring.

Tex Geddes, who had been my fellow harpoon-gunner in the Island of Soay Shark Fisheries, had come over to visit me from Soay, which he had bought when the venture was over. He left his boat anchored in the bay before the house, and we found so much to talk about that it was late at night when he remembered the time. The curtains were drawn and the lamps lit, and we had no knowledge of anything strange taking place in the outside world. Tex went out of the door in front of me, and I was still inside when I heard his voice.

'For Christ's sake! This must be the end of the world—they're shooting down the moon with Sputniks or something!'

Over his shoulder I looked out upon a sky that seemed, indeed, alight with some awful doom. We were standing, it appeared, under a stupendous conical canopy, in the arena, perhaps, of a cosmic circus, where infinitely far overhead a multi-coloured tent of light hung from a single point; or a tremendous magnification of a sight familiar during the war, when one stood at the centre of a circle from all of whose circumference searchlights were trained upon a single aircraft. But now the beams of the searchlights were each miles wide, shot with red and purple and green and blue, sheets of ice and of fire moving and merging with a terrible and remote grandeur.

Here and there the rays were interrupted and jagged, like the splintered wood of a snapped plank, but they soared up always towards that central point to join a coppery, dully-glowing ring of light. As we watched, the colours began to slide and to change; now the whole northern sky was red, while to the west it became a cold splendour of glacial green. Of all the natural sights that I have seen it was at the same time the most beautiful and the most terrible; it awoke in me some ancient racial animism, so that I felt that I could throw myself prostrate to worship and to placate.

In the autumn I made another attempt to acquire an otter, but by now with diminishing hope. A friend arranged to import, through a London dealer, two Indian Clawless otters; he was to keep one and I the other. They were described as being young and tame, a male and a female.

They were due to arrive at London Airport at about one o'clock in the morning, and such was our anxiety for their welfare that we were there to meet them. There was, however, no trace of them, and, reflecting that they were consigned to a dealer to whom they represented hard cash, we returned to bed. We telephoned to the dealer as soon as his premises were open, and were told that the otters had arrived and would be ready for collection at any time after two o'clock. We got there, more from eagerness than from any suspicion, at one-thirty; the crate was standing still unopened, as it had stood since the small hours of the morning. The two occupants were feeble, shivering, soaked in their own dung and urine, and almost too weak to stand. They died early the next day, mine in the new zoo hospital, and my friend's in his wife's lap; she had sat up all night trying to coax the pathetic little creature back to life.

It is, of course, precisely those people who find such incidents the most repugnant that by their patronage keep alive the nauseating market in wild animals, and after this I was determined that I would try no more importing of otters through normal channels.

These misfortunes might in themselves have deterred one less obsessed than I, but there was yet another in store, more tantalizing even than its predecessors, for this time all obstacles seemed already to have been surmounted. A veterinary officer from Singapore presented a hand-reared, house-living pet otter to an English zoo. The news of this action reached me immediately, and I at once offered an exchange for the abominable Kiko, whose market value was some four times that of the otter. My offer was accepted in writing, and I travelled south from Camusfeàrna to take delivery. During the twenty-four hours occupied by my journey, however, a friend of mine, all unaware of the trans-action, set about trying to obtain the otter for me, and to this end contacted the previous owner, who was spending a brief holiday in the north of England. For some reason this gentleman was determined that his pet should remain behind bars (with no more water, incidentally, than it could drink); and there, owing to the resulting fracas, and a regrettable timidity on the part of officials of the zoo concerned, it remains to this day.

After this third disappointment I made up my mind to rear a cub in Scotland, and with that end in view I returned to Camus-feàrna, for a prolonged stay, in the spring of 1959.

I had been there for no more than a week when there occurred by far the strangest episode in the saga of my efforts to replace Mijbil, a coincidence so extravagant, partaking so insolently of the world of fiction, that had it been unwitnessed or in another land I should hesitate to record it.

On 19th April I motored to the station, thirty-odd miles away, to meet an arriving guest, a foundation guest, as it were, who over many visits had constructed much of the Camusfeàrna furniture, and who with me had watched the house grow from an empty shell. I arrived very early in the village, to do some necessary shopping, and had lunch in the hotel, a large and exceedingly glossy hotel that caters for the most moneyed element of the tourist trade; in the summer it is loud with Cadillacs and transatlantic accents. Now, however, it was comparatively empty; and on falling into conversation with the hall porter I found that we had many acquaintances in common. He remembered my shark-fishing boat the *Sea Leopard*; we shared affectionate memories of Captain Robertson of the island steamer *Lochmor*, who, because of a voice pitched in an almost supersonic key, had been commonly known as Squeaky.

We exchanged stories about Squeaky, and it transpired that I knew one that he had never heard. It dated from the war years; Squeaky had been sailing northwards from Barra in a thick white mist, and there was among his passengers a certain admiral, spending his leave in the Hebrides. Peering from the boat-deck into the enveloping white screen, the admiral thought the ship on a course to lead her into a minefield, and as the minutes passed and the *Lochmor* churned on unheedingly he grew more and more apprehensive. At length his alarm became so acute that he decided to beard the captain on the bridge. The two had never met, and Squeaky was quite unaware that he was carrying a high-ranking naval officer. Gazing glassily ahead with his remarkably protuberant blue eyes, and dreaming perhaps of happy deals in coupon-free Harris tweed at the northern extremity of his run, he was suddenly outraged to observe standing at his elbow a stocky little man in a rain-coat and a Homburg hat. Squeaky was an habitually irascible man, and he exploded.

'Ket off my plutty pridge, you pugger!' he shouted in a voice like that of an angry wren.

The admiral remembered that he was in civilian clothes, apologised, and introduced himself. Squeaky, though by nature no respecter of persons, was impressed.

'An Atmiral, is it? And what could I be toing for you, Atmiral?'

'Well—Captain Robertson—I wondered whether you would be kind enough to give me our position.'

'Position? Ach, well, we're chust here or hereabouts.'

'No, no, Captain, I meant our position on the chart.'

'Is it a chart?' shrilled Squeaky. 'I haven't seen a chart for forty years!'

The admiral was insistent. 'Ach, well, Atmiral, if you're so keen to be seeing a chart, come down to my capin and have a wee tram, and we'll see what we can find you.'

The two went below to the captain's cabin, and after the 'wee tram' Squeaky began to rout about in his chart drawer. There were charts of the Indian Ocean and the China Sea, charts of Polar seas and of the Caribbean, of the English Channel and the Skagerrak; at last, seemingly at the very bottom of the drawer, he discovered a chart of the Minch. He spread this on the table, adjusted his spectacles, and at length planted a stubby forefinger a few miles north of Eriskay.

'Well, Atmiral, it's hereabouts we are, and this is our course northwards.'

The admiral stared ominously at a sprinkling of black dots right in the ship's path. 'What,' he asked bleakly, 'are these?'

Squeaky peered. 'Those plack tots? Well, if they're rocks we're puggered for sure, but if they're what I *think* they are, which is fly-shit, we're right as rain!'

I have digressed to recount the whole of this anecdote, partly because it is irresistible, and partly because the sharing of this joke and of other memories with the hall-porter had a direct bearing upon the dream-like happenings of two hours later. Had we not in those few minutes discovered the bond of mutual friends and recollections, those extraordinary events would never have taken place.

I met my guest on the station platform, and we returned to the hotel for what Squeaky would have called a 'wee tram' before setting off for Camusfeàrna. We sat in the sun-lounge that over-looks the sea, but we were well back from the window, and out of sight of the gravel sweep beyond the glass. Suddenly the hall porter came running over to us from the hall.

'Mr. Maxwell!' he called. 'Mr. Maxwell! Come quick to the door and tell me what's this strange beast outside—quick!'

I have an open mind on the subject of so-called telepathy and extra-sensory perception in general; I have had one or two curious experiences, but none quite as strange as the overwhelming and instant certainty that I felt then of what I was going to see. Whether that certainty communicated itself from me to my guest, or whether he had a separate moment of clairvoyance, he too had a sudden and vivid knowledge of what was outside the door.

Four people were walking past the hotel, making for a car parked near to the jetty. At their heels lolloped a large, sleek otter, of a species that I had never seen, with a silvery-coloured head and a snow-white throat and chest. I had a deep feeling of unreality, of struggling in a dream.

I rushed up to the party, and began to jabber, probably quite incoherently, about Mijbil and how he had been killed, and about how time and time again my efforts to find a successor had been frustrated at the eleventh hour. I must have been talking a great deal, because what they were saying in reply took a long time to sink in, and when it did the sense of dreaming increased almost to the point of vertigo.

'. . . only eight months old and always been free, house trained, comes and goes as she likes . . . brought her up myself with a bottle. In six weeks we've got to go back to West Africa, so it looked like a zoo or nothing—what else could we do? Everyone admires her, but when they come to the point of actually owning her they all shy off. . . . Poor Edal, it was breaking my heart. . . .'

We were sitting on the steps of the hotel by this time, and the otter was nuzzling at the nape of my neck—that well-remembered, poignant touch of hard whiskers and soft face-fur.

By the time I had taken in what her owners, Dr. Malcolm Macdonald and his wife, from Torridon, were saying, the party had dwindled by two; it transpired that the only reason why they had been in the village at all was to give a lift to two foreign girl hikers whose destination it was. And the only reason that I was there was to meet my guest, and the only reason that the Macdonalds and I had met at all was that two hours earlier I had made the acquaintance of the hall porter and exchanged reminiscences about Squeaky Robertson. I had not sat near enough to the window to see the otter for myself, and if he had not called me they would have passed by the hotel and gone home to Torridon, and I should have finished my drink ten minutes later and gone home to Camusfeàrna.

Ten days later Edal became mine, and there was once more an otter at Camusfeàrna, playing in the burn and sleeping before the hearth.

12

Malcolm Macdonald has set down for me the circumstances of Edal's early life, and the chain of events that led, on his side, to the strange climax of our meeting, the meeting of the only man in the British Isles who was trying desperately to find a home for a pet otter with the only man who was searching, with equal desperation, for an otter.

'She came on the 23rd of August, 1958.

'For the past year we had been living, my wife Paula and I, on a mature rubber plantation in the Niger Delta region of West Africa. Our nearest town was Sapele, two miles away and across the Benin river. The house we lived in was old, and built in the rambling barn-like style of half a century ago. It stood in a compound which generations of planters had filled with a profusion of flowering shrubs and fruit trees. We shared it with a motley collection of animal waifs and strays, and in their company we were never lonely.

'Paula had been shopping in Sapele that morning, and she came back from the riverside like the Pharaoh's daughter with a little bundle in her arms.

' "Just look what I've got!"

'The bundle parted and there was a plump broad silvery muzzle spiked with stiff translucent whiskers. Two hazy puppy eyes were struggling to open.

'We gazed down on her enraptured and smoothed her velvety coat.

'Under the funny flat face a little pink mouth appeared with brand-new needlepoints of teeth. It emitted an astonishingly loud demand to be fed. While Paula set off on a frantic rush to collect feeding-bottle and teat, milk and boiled water, I tried to comfort this strange new waif.

'Priscilla came up and looked on in calm enquiry. Priscilla was a half-Alsatian bitch. The composition of the other half was open to speculation and she was about a year old. Very soon after our arrival at Sapele she had turned up from God knows where, a spindly-legged, pot-bellied, thoroughly ugly and very sick puppy. We took her in, and she recovered to stay with us and grow into a beautiful animal, a constant friend and a natural guard dog.

'Now Priscilla took upon herself a most important function, which was probably vital to the successful rearing of the new-comer.

'Responding to the little creature's cries for help, gently but firmly and with a somewhat officious air, she nuzzled the cloth aside and licked. She was rewarded with a positive explosion of wind and a stream of excrement. The cub's cries became less desperate, though they persisted until feeding was accomplished, and Priscilla sat back and looked smug.

'Disappointment is all too often the lot of people who attempt to rear very young animals, and frequently it is due to lack of the very necessary maternal service which Priscilla so kindly provided. In the absence of an obliging bitch gentle massage with a moist finger will serve.

'In due course the bottle was prepared. Paula took the cub into the crook of her arm and offered her the rubber teat; as soon as she tasted the milk she sucked avidly, but she was soon satisfied, taking little more than an ounce, and fell into a deep contented sleep.

'While she slept we took stock of the situation.

'At the end of her morning's shopping in Sapele Paula had noticed several Africans standing arguing around one of their number who held a box containing, it seemed to her at first, a couple of very young puppies. Their talk caught her interest.

' "Which kind of beef dis?" said one.

' "Na tree-bear," answered another.

' "At all," said a third. "Dis na rabbit." (Rabbit is the local name for a species of big rat.) A fourth was emphatic in his disbelief.

' "Na lie," he said.

'Paula's curiosity overcame her and she went to see for herself. At the same time a senior African joined the group. "This be the piccin of water-dog," he intoned, settling the controversy for good.

'It transpired that two young fishermen had come upon the holt in a river bank and heard the cubs inside. So the cubs were dug out, and it is certain that if they had been old enough to show the least hostility they would have been done to death there and then. However, being obviously harmless and too small to be of much consequence as "beef" they were carried off unharmed to Sapele. It is well known there that some Europeans have a kind of "craze for head" which induces them to part with ludicrously large sums of money for useless beasts—particularly if the beasts are small and helpless and sure to die if left.

'There were two cubs, a male and a female. The female was larger and lighter in colour than the male. It seemed somewhat stronger and more advanced, too, in that its eyes were beginning to open. Both cubs were a silvery-grey colour, lighter at the head, with creamy white throats and "shirt-fronts". At each side the white was sharply divided from the grey at a line which extended from the angle of the jaw to the shoulder. Their tails were no thicker than an ordinary pencil.

'After much palaver Paula secured possession of the female cub for the single pound note she had with her and extracted a promise that should the other cub not be sold to a European within a very short time it would be brought to our house. The other cub was, in fact, bought by an amateur animal collector who, a few weeks later, took his entire collection to a zoo in England which he held in high esteem. The cub, however, died later of a cerebral haemorrhage.

'Now we had an otter to bring up. Our knowledge of otters was virtually nil. They are rarely seen in West Africa, for cover is abundant and they are mainly nocturnal in habit; once, however, we had had the good fortune to see a pair of Cameroons otters.

We were staying at an oil-palm plantation in the southern part of the British Cameroons, and one evening we stood upon a promontory of high ground at a remote edge of the plantation. Below us on our left there was a big river running in spate. From its far bank the dense black rain forest stretched for endless unknown miles into the heart of Africa. Directly below us, from a waterfall to our right, a clear stream flowed through deep pools to join the river. The brief equatorial dusk was beginning.

'Among the rocks below the waterfall two brown figures were playing, indistinct at that distance. For several minutes they sported together, sometimes upright, sometimes rolling on the smooth bare rocks. Then taking cleanly to the water, they swam with magnificent sinuous grace through the clear calm pools a hundred feet below us. Unmistakably otters they were then, but so big that our native otters must seem pygmies by comparison. They were not less than five feet from nose to tip of tail, lithe and powerful, a breath-taking sight.

'We wondered if our little cub might grow so big. We guessed then that she was two weeks old; now we think that she had been born a month.

'Two hours after her first meal with us she wakened and struggled free of the towel which was her temporary bed. Using her stubby loose-jointed limbs as oars she rowed herself along on her sleek belly. She was pleased to receive our attentions and took another small feed, made up of one part of ordinary canned evaporated milk with two parts of boiled and cooled water added. This was a pretty strong mixture and when, as did occur in the first two or three weeks, the cub had diarrhoea we diluted it by simple rule of thumb reckoning. In any case we came to the conclusion that some looseness of the bowels with mucus is normal to an infant otter. The mixture was served at a little above body heat, i.e. perceptibly warm to the touch at elbow or back of wrist.

'In the first two or three weeks she slept most of the time, as infants do. She grew rapidly, and almost with every awakening one could see the development of her strength and co-ordination of movement. In all five senses her range of perception increased in proportion; her eyes opened wider and rounder and their smokiness cleared. Movements attracted her; she came to recognize her bottle and would stretch out her hands to hold it.

'They were fascinating, those hands. The stubby fingers were strong and mobile and only slightly webbed. At the tip of each pink finger there was a tiny depression, the vestigial representative of a claw. Her hands were important to her; she used them to investigate every new object, and as she grew older they developed amazing dexterity.

'Edal, as we called her, had an instinct for cleanliness, and always on waking she would struggle away from her bed for toilet purposes. We occupied only the cool upper floor of our house, and feared for her safety, so we made her a day-bed in a beer crate. Crumpled copies of the airmail *Daily Telegraph* made an excellent disposable, absorbent base, and soft cotton cloths made the bed proper. There she had comfort and freedom from draughts and room to move about and keep dry.

'The nights at that season were chilly, and when we went to bed she slept in a nest between our pillows. There was many a frantic rush when a squeaky "Whee, whee" proclaimed that she was stirring.

'For the first two or three days we fed her two-hourly, with one or more feeds in the night as she demanded them. And those feeds had to be just right. An indignant crescendo "Wheeeeeeeee" soon told us if the bottle were cold. Time passed; the intervals between feeds extended to four hours, and the night feeds were stopped. The quantity she took at each feed increased to six ounces.

'When feeding, Edal liked to lie on her back in the crook of one's arm. Tightly holding the neck of the bottle she would squirm with pleasure as she sucked, thrusting back hard with her little round head. Priscilla and the kitten Stinky Pooh and sometimes the elegant black tom-cat Sooty would gather round, waiting for the milk that would be left when Edal was satisfied. Squeezing the polythene feeding-bottle produced a fine stream of milk. Stinky Pooh was expert at catching the jet; with tongue oscillating briskly and ears pinned back she never missed a drop.

Poor Priscilla just could not compete. With her tongue flapping wildly and her bottom shuffling with embarrassment she would get milk up her nose, into her eyes, anywhere but into her big mouth. Sooty was none too clever either and would stalk away angrily, flipping a disdainful paw.

'Edal now slept all night in her own little bed beside ours. At about six o'clock the first houseboy to come in would carry her out to join Priscilla for a short time, whilst her first feed and our own morning tea were prepared. Throughout this time Priscilla devotedly assisted with her personal hygiene, and I am sorry to say that Edal responded only with indignation and base ingratitude.

'We were particularly pleased with our "boys". They had been accustomed enough to tending our animals, but to Edal they became almost as devoted as we.

'We were more than amply rewarded for those broken nights. As she grew and took on her proper otter shape and became an active member of the household she was delightful. By the end of September she was about eighteen inches long, a scampering, merry little otter cub.

'When first introduced to the bath Edal yelled with fright. It took a great deal of talking and soothing to convince her that an otter should like water, but soon she found that it was great fun to splash about in an inch or two of cool water. Not bad stuff to drink, either.

'Over a period of days we made her baths gradually deep enough for real swimming. With a supporting hand at first she learned that she could swim. Industriously paddling round she would look up with the most comical expression. Well! Just look at me!

'As we laughed back at her she positively grinned. "Wheee-eee". This was living.

'How she loved that bath. She learned to swim under water and do corkscrew rolls. With a thrust of her broad webbed feet she would lunge forward out of the water and belly-flop. She loved, too, to play peek-a-boo over the edge of the bath, diving quick as a flash. She gathered a collection of bath toys, all sorts of odds and ends, though her favourite was a plastic pint measure.

First she would sink it; then, drawing a deep breath, she would thrust her head into it and swim with it clattering around the bath.

'When she tired she would come to the side to be lifted out and dried. Sometimes she would take over long in tiring and the bath attendant for the occasion would take the plug out. This was an eternal mystery to Edal. Where did that water go? She would thrust her muzzle into the hole, poke her fingers through the grid, sit on it. Finally, the water gone, she would peer wistfully after it and look up enquiringly. Then, accepting the situation with her usual good humour, she would come and be dried.

'She loved laughter and would positively join in, grinning and prancing.

'Her basic conversational vocabulary was a high-pitched whistling "Whee". With loud and soft, short and long and other variations of "Whees" she had quite a lot to say and said it. We came to understand much of it. Two expressions in particular we knew. "Wheeeee-uk" said "I want some water in the bath," and several anxious chirping "whees" suggested a swift trip to the garden.

'She had to be introduced gently to the out-of-doors. It was just too BIG out there. From her lavatory patch she would toddle anxiously back to the safety of the doorway. There she would pause and turn, head down and wary, as ancestral memories stirred of the lurking enemies of her race. Then her white throat would gleam as her head rose high and she would stand poised with one arm flexed for a final reassuring look round.

'She very quickly learned to scramble up the stairs to our living-room, one laborious step after another, and was always patently glad to be back. This was her home, and she accepted us as her parents who loved her and laughed with her and provided all she required. And her greatest requirement was our company. In her waking hours she would never willingly let us out of her sight. It was a requirement we found easy to fulfil, for we never tired of hers.

'Her playmates lived here too. Priscilla played with Edal kindly and patiently, but it was in Stinky Pooh that she found a real kindred spirit. Stinky Pooh was one of those starry-eyed fluffy sedate-little-girl kittens who surprise you by behaving like tomboys. She and Edal would roll and tumble in ferocious mock battles, and their greatest joy was a friendly squabble over a ball of screwed-up paper.

'The grey parrot wasn't really a playmate. A glutton for petting himself he was jealous of the little stranger. He had come to us as "dash"—pidjin English for a present—and, not knowing at first that he was a cock bird, we called him Polly. As the youngsters roistered on the floor Polly would watch them with his pale cold eyes. Like a crotchety old Giles schoolmaster he would hobble across the room and, pecking them indiscriminately, would take away their paper ball. Carrying it to his perch by the window he would moodily tear it to shreds.

'Poor Polly; when Edal grew a little older he met his deserts. One day he fled squawking while she, munching on a mouthful of red tail feathers, registered sheer delight.

'We kept three monkeys then. Two were mere lodgers whom we looked after whilst their mistress was away, and they spent nearly all their time in a big wire cage in the compound. The third was a Mona monkey we had reared ourselves.

'She had been found clinging to the thick back hair of her mother's corpse. The native hunter who slew the mother for sale as "beef" brought the pathetic infant to our house. Paula, ever an easy victim to this form of moral blackmail, gave him a few shillings for her. She was a tiny wizened creature, almost bald and toothless, with terror standing in her shiny brown eyes, and her little body was chafed and sore with the coarse raffia string that bound her. It is a hard-hearted person indeed who will not spare a shilling or two to take such unfortunates from their pedlars— if only to grant them the mercy of dying in peace.

'We called the tiny monkey Oweenk, from her own plaintive cry. She snuggled into Paula's neck, grateful for a little love and protection.

'Paula fed her on very dilute milk from an eye dropper and she thrived. By the time Edal came Oweenk was nearly a foot tall and a pain in the neck. We could allow her full liberty for only a short time each day and then only under close supervision. She wore a small dog-collar around her waist and spent the greater part of each day on a long string in the garden.

'These monkeys are very affectionate in their own crazy way. They love to cling to one and hate to be alone. But they are full of sin. At liberty in a house they leave a trail of devastation, and little can be done to teach them good behaviour. In illustration of this there is a story of a man who set about house-training one. Diligently, when the monkey messed, he would seize it, slap its backside, and toss it out of the window. After some weeks his efforts bore fruit. The monkey would mess on the floor, slap its own backside, and jump out of the window.

'When Oweenk was first allowed to meet the toddling Edal she danced and chattered with delight. She cuddled Edal in her arms and searched in her fur—much to Edal's chagrin—and wailed when they were separated. All too soon, monkey-wise, the loving turned to mischievous teasing and eventually they became enemies.

'To me the much-vaunted human affinity of the monkey wears thin in the presence of an otter, and as these two young creatures grew up together the comparison of their behaviour made a fascinating study.

'Edal's tactile handling of objects contrasted with Oweenk's frenzied manipulations; her joyful play with the monkey's staccato caperings. Gay friendliness contrasted with urchin familiarity, and innocent interest with acquisitive seeking. The contrasts were legion, but they all favoured the otter.

'With the month of October came tribulation. Edal shed her front incisor milk teeth and little buds of new white enamel appeared in their place. At the same time she became dissatisfied with her bottle. One afternoon when I went to the kitchen refrigerator for a cold drink she tried to scramble into it, snorting loudly and greatly excited. The cook had left some herring roes there and Edal wanted them. I cut them into strips for her and she ate them all. Soon the mystified manager of the Sapele Kingsway Shop wanted to know why on earth we wanted so many of his cold-store herrings. Edal was weaned.

'With proper parental pride we applauded these events, but then her eye teeth, the canines of her upper jaw, began to give her much trouble, and our jubilation changed to concern. For a week and more she was fretful and nagged with pain. She would lie on the floor or in her bed "wheeing" plaintively and rummaging in her mouth with her hands. She would come and plead for help and comfort, gnawing one's fingers. At night she sought comfort in Paula's bed; her sleep was fitful and disturbed, and many times a day she called to be put in the bath to cool her fevered body and soothe her aching mouth. Her body lost its sleek roundness and her fur its silvery sheen. She ate little and that without enthusiasm, and blankly refused to return to bottle feeds. And yet, in her easier moments, she would find a little toy and feebly play.

'Nor was this all. At the same time we were horrified to see that her right eye was badly inflamed, the cornea blue and swollen. But this condition too was transitory, for it responded satisfactorily to an eye-drop formula and after a few more wretched days the tooth on the left side came away. She took on a new lease of life, eating prodigiously, playing gaily, and sleeping soundly. She grew sleek again, and her coat gleamed. There were minor recurrences of her eye trouble into the early part of November; then the last recalcitrant tooth separated, and her childish ailments were over.

'We engaged a local native fisherman, an old man with a permanently disgruntled expression. His fish he caught in basket traps set overnight, and each morning he brought them alive in a bucket from the Jameson River. Edal had usually demolished them all by night, and we supplemented her diet with butter, eggs, and fresh liver.

'The only people I met who had seen otters, other than the nocturnal fishermen, were workers upon an oil-palm plantation which I visited. Part of the plantation lay close to the Benin river bank and sometimes at dawn they surprised "water-dogs" foraging for the oil and vitamin-rich palm fruit. Edal, however, preferred butter.

'The diet we gave her seemed satisfactory, for she grew well, and was always bursting with high good humour. Nothing escaped her interest, and everything was examined for its possibilities as a plaything. Bottles were just made to be rolled upon and a box of matches was treasure-trove. She appeared to derive enormous satisfaction from scattering a boxful of matches and then packing them, one by one, into the toe of a slipper. Finally she would thrust her arm through the cover of the box and wear it like an outsize bangle. All this made life pretty lively when I settled down to relax with a drink and cigarettes at night.

'Her appetite was astounding. She took a great interest in our own meals and attended regularly at table for titbits. She rejected all cooked meats except pork and ham, liked some vegetables, especially runner beans, enjoyed pastry, and was frantically fond of ice-cream. She would take a piece in both hands and cram it into her mouth, making ecstatic little mewing noises and getting thoroughly messy. When offered a tasty morsel she really wanted she would moan softly and "hurrrh" through her nose before taking it.

'She drank frequently and spent a great deal of her time in the bathroom, for when not actually in the bath she liked to take her day-time naps there. She liked a towel to sleep on, and if one were not already provided she would help herself, pulling one down from the towel-rail and dragging it off to a quiet corner. Bunching it up beneath her she would worry at it until she found a suitable part to suck; then she would suck at it with tremendous fervour, eyes shut tight, mewing and snuffling and waggling her rump until she fell asleep.

'By now the stairs were no longer an obstacle to her, and she could go out and in at will. From Priscilla she learned to recognize the sound of my car, and when I returned home in the afternoons they both would come rushing out in a riotous welcome, competing to be first. Edal would seize Priscilla by a hind paw, making her turn around, then dash between her legs to gain a yard or so.

'She joined our evening walks with Priscilla and Oweenk and the cats. When we left the house she became very wary, staying close to heel and snorting in alarm at any sudden movement, with an inborn awareness, it seemed, of the persecution to which her race is subject.

'Even at home she was apt to wail and squirm with apprehension when a stranger entered the house, and she would have to be reassured with a few soothing words and the touch of a hand, for she looked to us at all times for protection and guidance.

'In nature she would have enjoyed a relatively long period of parental care; now the responsibility was ours to see that she did not want for understanding and sympathy.

'So long as she felt safe she was the most charmingly amiable and playful of creatures, but there was nothing submissive about her friendliness; it was always on a basis of mutual esteem. She made many friends, for there were few visitors to our house who were not captivated by her, and she was gentle and affectionate with children.

'The New Year came, and we began to be anxious for the future of our protégée. We were due to return to the United Kingdom at the beginning of March, and although several kind people offered to keep her we hated the thought of abandoning her. She had no tradition of domesticity behind her, and, although her wild instincts were so well reconciled with her life with us, she might not be able to establish the same harmony with others. She was still very young; her reactions in those circumstances were unpredictable, for she was deeply attached to us, as indeed were we to her. At that time we were half-persuaded that the best eventual home for her would be a good zoo, where she would receive the best of care from professional animal keepers, but we have since been sadly disillusioned on that score.

'One afternoon I was to meet Paula at the Sapele ferry. Edal followed me to the car so I took her along with some idea of accustoming her to travelling. At first she was nervous in the car, clinging anxiously to my neck and pressing hard against me. I drove slowly down to the waterside, talking to her all the while, and persuading her that she had nothing to fear.

'We sat waiting near to the ferry pier, at peace with the world. An African girl with a basket of peppers on her head sauntered by singing.

'As she saw Edal the basket teetered and her eyes dilated wide. She yelled.

' "Yah! Look um! Look de beef!"

'In seconds a jabbering crowd surrounded us.

' "Eh! Look um!"

' "Look 'e'n teeth!"

' "Dem pass dog own!"

' " 'E fit to bite man proppah!"

' "How 'e no de bite white man?"

' "Ah! Dis na docitah. I t'ink say 'e gie um injection."

'A seamy faced character in tattered shorts, evidently a fisherman, pushed into the crowd.

' "Eh Heh! Na watta–dog! 'E keel feesh fo' watta! 'E bad fo' we! If 'e get chance 'e savvy bite man too much!"

'I had started the engine, and as I let in the clutch our knowledgeable friend was expounding the culinary properties of young otters.

' "As 'e dead now, 'e sweet to chop. . . ."

'It was decided that Edal should come with us. Polly was to come as well. In the short time remaining I obtained the import permit from London and booked aircraft space. Edal was required to travel in a ventilated box and Polly in a light travelling cage.

'We started the journey on an appallingly hot day in early March with a flight from Benin to Lagos. The small aircraft was like an oven in the blistering mid-day sun. Throughout the flight the air was turbulent, and the plane was tossed about like a small boat in a storm. We were terribly anxious for Edal.

'At Lagos she was unconscious and on the point of death. We rushed her to our rest house; her limp body was fiercely hot, her breathing intermittent and gasping, and her heart fluttered feebly as she struggled for life in the last stage of heat exhaustion. We placed her on her back in the bath in an inch of cool water, moistened her parched mouth, and bathed her limbs with iced water from the refrigerator.

'When her condition became a little less desperate we placed her on a wet towel under the fan in our shaded bedroom. While

Paula went into the city for some essential shopping I stayed beside Edal and went on bathing her and moistening her mouth with iced water. Very slowly the raging heat left her; she breathed more steadily, and her heart beat less frantically; then she lapsed into a deep sleep.

'In the evening I had to leave the room for a few minutes. The closing of the door must have disturbed her, for when I returned she had crept under a chair where she crouched bewildered and fearful. As I knelt to speak to her, relief and recognition shone in her eyes; weakly she reached up to cling to my neck, and mewed and nuzzled against my face.

'The following evening we joined a B.O.A.C. Stratocruiser bound for London. Edal was rested and well again, and I had given her a tranquillizing pill. She was to travel in a pressurized compartment below the forward passenger cabin. There was a refuelling stop at Kano before the long night flight across the Sahara and on to Rome.

'When we took her out at Kano we were delighted and relieved to find her sleepy and quite unperturbed. She followed us non-chalantly to the airport buildings, where she made friends with the aircraft's captain, and in the middle of a plot of grass—to call it a lawn would be flattery—she found a watering point and played happily with the jet.

'We gave her another tranquillizer and she must have slept throughout the night, for we heard no more of her until we were over the Channel and descending towards London. Then she began to whistle and cry; the steward was sympathetic but Edal's compartment was inaccessible in flight.

'In the Customs hall there was the usual milling throng of sleepy passengers and bustling baggage porters. A saturnine Customs Officer looked through our sheaf of import and export licences and veterinary certificates and chalked our baggage without spoken comment. Friends were waiting outside with a car. Polly was quite debonair, fluttering his flame-red tail and wolf-whistling wickedly at the passers by. A voice called, "Look out mate, yer arse is on fire!"

'Edal was in a pitiful state, thirsty and hungry and worn out from her struggles to escape; her fingers were raw and bleeding and there was an angry worn patch on her muzzle. Her ordeal was nearly over now, but there remained an overnight train journey to Inverness.

'At Euston the guard was understanding and helpful. He could not allow Edal to join us in the sleeping accommodation but he took her box into his own warm section of the van where a stove burned, and we were duly grateful.

'At Inverness the morning was crisp and bright. I took delivery of my car at the station and we headed for the country, pausing only to buy some fish for her. The day was fine and clear with the warmth of spring in the air, and we dawdled along towards the mountains of the western seaboard, revelling in the pastel highland hues after Africa's garish colours, and stopping often to let Edal investigate her new homeland. She was happy to be free with us again, and bore us no ill will for the horrors of the journey. She travelled well by car but was a restless passenger, scrambling from side to side to peer out of the windows.

'In the next few weeks, as the spring unfolded, I explored anew with Edal the sea-shore and the mountain burns that I had known in my childhood. Although she had recoiled at first from the biting chill of the water, our colder climate seemed to agree with her. On the ebb tides we dug the succulent clams from the sands and she learned to hunt for crabs and cobbler-fish among the rocks and tangle. She was still growing fast. When we left Nigeria she was three feet long and weighed fifteen pounds; by May she had grown by ten pounds and a good half dozen inches, and was immensely strong.

'Those were happy weeks indeed, but we were due to go to Ghana in June and again we began to worry about her future. Dearly as we loved to have her with us, the necessity for many more thousands of miles of travel made parting with her, at least for a time, inevitable. We were anxious to see her properly settled and in good hands before the time came for us to go.

'One beautiful morning in late April we set out to motor to the village of Plockton, near Kyle of Lochalsh. For most of the previous evening we had discussed what we might best do for

Edal, and were miserable at the prospect of parting with her. We had been urged to lodge her in a particular zoo, and had, been assured that she would be given every care and attention there. Still we recoiled from the idea, and could reach no decision.

'On the road to Plockton two foreign girls on a youth hostelling holiday hitched a lift with us. They wanted to go to Skye, and since the ferry was but a few miles off our route we elected to take them there.

'We made our usual intermittent progress, stopping every twenty miles or so to let Edal out for a while. In the early afternoon we stopped at the Lochalsh Hotel and wandered along the terrace, looking across to the hills of Skye. The gods were smiling on us that day, for they had taken the nagging question of Edal's future into their own hands. As we came abreast of the hotel door a figure bolted from it like a ferreted rabbit, laying a trail of whisky from the glass clutched forgotten in his hand, his whole attention fixed delightedly and incredulously on Edal.'

13

NOTHING WAS decided at that first meeting; Edal's owners not
unnaturally wanted to satisfy themselves that this extraordinary
coincidence was all it seemed on the surface, and that she would
find with me the home they wanted for her. They promised to
write during the next few days; Edal jumped into their car with
the ease of familiarity, and as they drove away she appeared
leaning far out of the passenger window, one hand delicately
shielding her windward ear.

A week later she visited Camusfeàrna for an afternoon; then,
after an interval of ten days Malcolm and Paula came to stay for a
week-end, to leave Edal with me when they went. I had not been
idle during those ten days; I was determined to repeat none of the
mistakes that had led, directly or indirectly, to Mij's death. I sent
to Malcolm Macdonald a harness that had been made for Mij
just before he was killed; with the help of Jimmy Watt I enclosed
the house with a fence that might not, perhaps, have foiled Mij,
but which would, I thought, be barrier enough to baffle this
apparently more docile, less self-willed creature if she should
think in the first days to seek her late foster parents; within these
confines we dug a pool and piped to it water that rose in a fountain jet appropriate to more formal surroundings. The entrance
to this enclosure, and thus to the house, we guarded by a double
gate, the lowermost wood of which met a sheet of metal sunk
into the ground against digging. I did not think that these precautions would be necessary for long; they were to make certain
that during the period when she would inevitably fret and believe
herself to belong elsewhere I should not lose her through any
fault of my own.

Even during that first week-end, while I was still a stranger to her and her surroundings were unfamiliar, I was so enchanted by Edal that I found it difficult to believe my own good fortune. Because she did not feel herself to be in her own home I was able to see in those first days only a fraction of her fascination, a mere corner of the picquant personality I came to know later, but I saw enough to know that if I had searched the world over I could have found no more perfect successor to Mijbil.

On the third day, while Edal was sleeping soundly on the sofa, Paula and Malcolm left silently. Our good-byes were hushed, almost tacit, both because we did not want to awaken that softly-breathing ball of fur, and because something of their own feeling of unhappiness and betrayal had communicated itself to me, and in my long-postponed moment of triumph I felt not jubilation but sadness for the sundered family.

After they had gone Jimmy and I sat beside Edal on the sofa, waiting miserably for her awakening and the panic that we thought would follow the realization of her abandonment. An hour passed, two, and still she slept on. Presently Morag arrived; the Macdonalds had called at Druimfiaclach as they left, and told her that Edal might feel less lost and despairing in feminine company. So we three sat silently and anxiously, as around a sick bed, and my thoughts wandered between the sleeping animal and her late owners, for I had recognized in them the same obsessional feeling for their otter as I had experienced for Mij, and for nothing in the world would I have changed places with them as they drove home desolate now.

When Edal awoke at last she appeared to notice little amiss. Paula's jersey lay beside her on the sofa, her own towel and toys were on the floor, and if she was aware of her owners' absence she was too well-mannered a guest to comment upon it so early. Also, as was to be expected, she got on extremely well with Morag.

It is time to give a more detailed description of Edal as she was when she came to me early in May 1959.

By far the strangest and most captivating aspect of her was that of her hands. Unlike Mij, whose forepaws were, despite the dexterity he contrived with them, true paws with wide connecting webs between the digits, hers were monkey-hands, unwebbed, devoid of so much as a vestige of nail, and nearly as mobile as a man's. With them she ate, peeled hard-boiled eggs, picked her teeth, arranged her bed, and played for hours with any small object that she could find.

Once in a hospital in Italy I watched a cripple child practising the use of artificial hands. She had before her a solitaire board and a numbered set of marbles; the holes were numbered too, but the marbles had been wrongly placed, and her task was to transpose them until each ball and socket corresponded. She worked with complete absorption, oblivious of onlookers, and with each passing minute she discovered new powers. Once, too, I had watched a ball juggler practising his act with the same withdrawn, inturned eye, the same absence of irritation or impatience at failure, the same apparent confidence of ultimate success.

Of both these Edal reminded me as she juggled with such small objects—marbles, clothes-pegs, matches, Biro pens—as could be satisfactorily contained within her small, prehensile grasp; she would lie upon her back passing them from hand to hand, or occasionally to the less adept grip of her webbed but almost nailless hind feet, working always with two or more objects at a time, gazing fixedly at them all the while, as though these extremities of hers were in some way independent of her and to be watched and wondered at. At moments it was clearly frustrating for her to require four feet upon which to walk, for she would retrieve a lost marble clutching it firmly in one hand—usually the right—and hobbling along upon her other three limbs.

Because, it seemed, of her delight in her own dexterity, it was her practice to insert her plaything of the moment into some container from which it had then to be extracted, a boot or a shoe for choice, and it mattered little to her whether this receptacle already contained a human foot. She would come hobbling across the room to me with some invisible treasure clenched in her right fist and thrust it into my shoe just below the ankle bone; on more than one occasion the foreign body thus introduced turned out

180

Edal when she first arrived

Lifting a glass net float from the water to play football

Playing with the jet of a garden hose

'An accomplishment probably unchallenged among wild animals—that of drinking milk from a spoon'

'She would pass about these pools where Mij had hunted before her'

Edal and her keeper at the waterfall

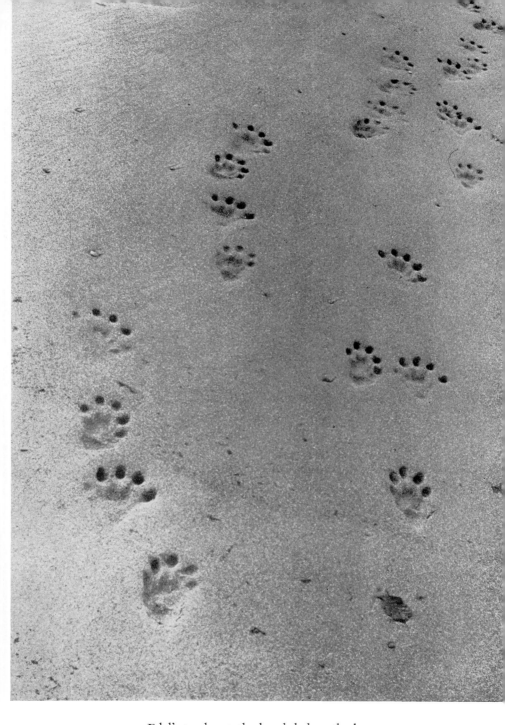

Edal's tracks on the beach below the house

A razor shell at the tide's edge

'Bouncing inboard with a flurry of aerated water'

(*above*)

The geese on one of the island beaches; Edal in the background

(*right*)

'The bigger dinghy dragged her moorings and stove a plank'; Edal caught a dab in the scuppers

During repairs to the old croft Edal proved herself quite
unafraid of ladders

Edal and Jimmy Watt on their morning walk

'A habit of gathering up this bib in her two hands and sucking it'

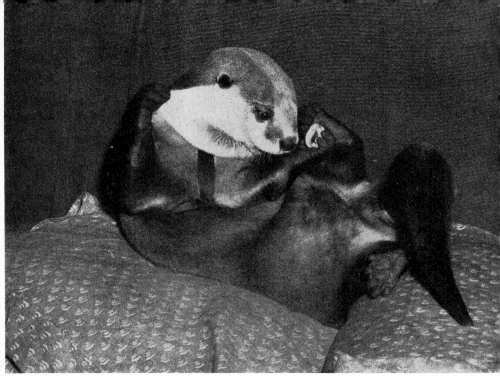

Edal juggling with a small piece of rubber tube from a Schnorkel mask

Concentration

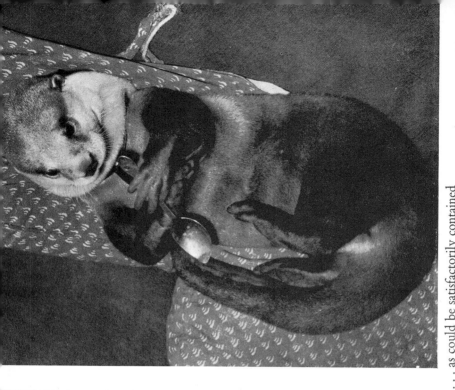

'She juggled with such small objects . . . as could be satisfactorily contained within her small, prehensile grasp'

Edal would appear to emulate
the Modigliani nude above her
self-chosen bed

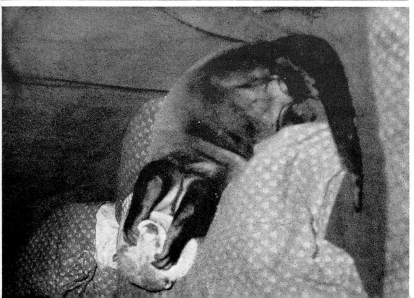

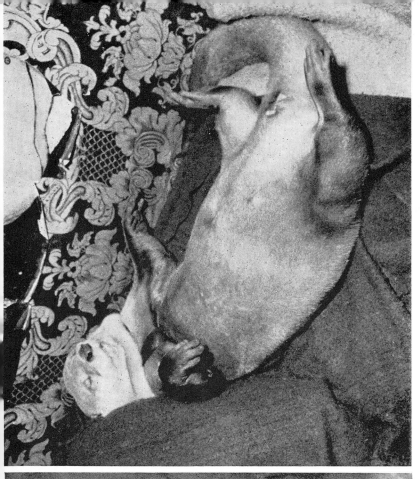

Replete with food and play

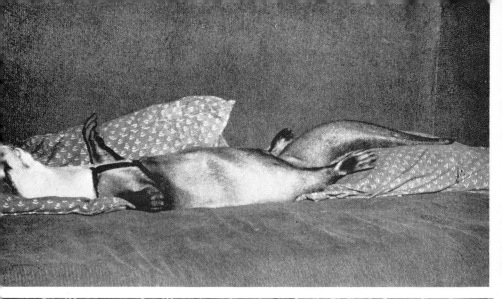

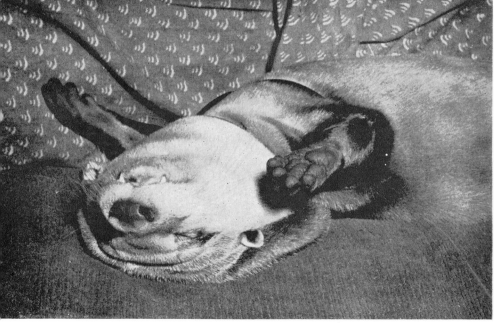

'The expression of tightly shut concentration that very small babies wear in sleep.' The lower photograph repays study the wrong way up

'To fly free and unafraid about Camusfeàrna . . . to hear in the dawn and the dusk the wild music of those voices'

'The wheeling silver-shouldered flight of the geese as they passed to alight ahead of us'

'A more detailed examination revealed the cat in the chimney'

Edal about her own pursuits in the Camusfeàrna bay

to be a large and lively black beetle. She was also an adept, if not entirely imperceptible, pickpocket; with impatiently fumbling fingers she would reach disconcertingly into the trouser pockets of any guest who sat down in the house, hardly waiting for an introduction before scattering the spoils and hurrying away with as much as she could carry. With these curious hands she could, too, throw such playthings as were small enough to be enclosed by her fingers. She had three ways of doing this; the most usual was a quick upward flick of the arm and forepart of the body as she held her clenched fist palm downward, but she would also perform a backward flick which tossed the object over her shoulder to land at her other side, and, on occasion, usually when in a sitting position with her back supported, she would throw overarm.

Like Mij, she was an ardent footballer, and would dribble a ball round the room for half an hour at a time, but here she had an additional accomplishment that Mij had not learned, for when she shot the ball wide or over-ran it she would sweep her broad tail round with a powerful scoop to bring it back within range of her feet.

For the rest she was a small, exceedingly heavy body inhabiting a rich fur skin many sizes too large for her. It cannot be described as a loose fit; it is not a fit at all. The skin appears to be attached to the creature inside it at six points only: the base of the nose, the four wrists or ankles, and the root of the tail. When lying at ease upon her back the surplus material may be observed disposed in heavy velvety folds at one or other side of her, or both; a slight pressure forward from the base of her neck causes the skin on her forehead to rise in a mountain of pleats like a furled plush curtain; when she stands upright like a penguin the whole garment slips downwards by its own inertia into heavy wrinkles at the base of her belly, giving her a non-upsettable, pear-shaped appearance.

She is thus able to turn, within surprisingly broad limits, inside her own skin, and should one attempt to pick her up by the scruff of the neck one is liable to find oneself gripping a portion of skin rightly belonging to some quite different part of her body, merely on temporary loan, so to speak, to the neck. The colour of the fur is the best guide to what really belongs where; her chest and throat are of yellow-tinged white—not pure white as I had thought when seeing her first in the sunshine—and here the pelt hangs in such positive bags of redundancy that she has a habit of gathering up this bib in her two hands and sucking it with an enjoyment that the fine plush texture makes wholly understandable. The bib is divided from a silvery, brocade-texture head by a sharp line of demarcation immediately below the ears; the body and the enormous tail are pale mauvish-brown, velvet above and silk below. Beyond the points of attachment at the four wrists the fur is of an entirely different character; it changes from velvet to satin, tiny, close-lying hairs that alter colour according to how the light falls upon them. The tightly gloved hands and the enormous fullness above the wrists give her the appearance of wearing heavy gauntlets; watching her lolloping out for her morning walk with Jimmy Watt I have thought that she resembled nothing so much as a very expensive woman taking no chances on the weather at a point-to-point meeting.

Her comparative babyhood, and her upbringing by human beings, had left some strange gaps in her abilities. To start with, she could not lap water or milk, but only drink from a dish as does a bird, lifting her head to allow the liquid to trickle down her throat, or sucking it noisily with a coarse, soup-drinking sound punctuated with almost vocal swallowing. She possessed, however, an accomplishment probably unchallenged among wild animals—that of drinking milk from a spoon. One had but to produce and exhibit a cup and spoon for her to clamber on to one's lap and settle herself with a heavy and confiding plump, head up and expectant. Then she opened her mouth and one poured the spoonfuls into it, while the soup noises reached a positive crescendo. At the end of this performance she would insist upon inspecting the cup to make certain that it was indeed empty; she would search into it with enquiring fingers and abstracted gaze; then, belching and hiccupping from time to time, she would lift the spoon out in one clenched hand and lie upon her back, licking and sucking it.

It came as a shock to me to discover that she was the most

precarious of swimmers. Even in the wild state otter cubs have little if any instinct for water, and their dam teaches them to swim against their better judgment, as it were, for they are afraid to be out of their depth. In the water Edal preferred to keep her feet either in surreptitious contact with the bottom or within easy reach of it, and nothing, at that time, would tempt her into deep water. Within these self-imposed limits, however, she was capable of a performance that even Mij might have envied; lying on her back she would begin to spin, if that is the correct word, to revolve upon her own axis, to pirouette in the horizontal plane, like a chicken on a spit that has gone mad. In this, as in the novelty of new aquabatic powers that she quickly learned, she took a profound delight, and if she had not yet apprehended that otters should swim under-water and only return to the surface for refreshment, she knew all the joys of a great disturbance upon it.

Her language was at first an enormous problem to me. While she shared a certain number of notes with Mij they were, whether by reason of her different species or because she had not been taught to speak by parent otters, used in so utterly different contexts as to produce, at the beginning, acute misunderstanding. Thus the singing hum that had proclaimed Mij's extreme anger she employed to ask for food that a human was holding, and she later learned to do this at request. Mij's interrogatory 'Hah?' was, with her, also a request for some piece of food held in the human hand, a confirmation that she had smelled it and found it acceptable. The high, snarling wail that had, very rarely, marked the end of Mij's patience and the probability of a bite, she produced in response to any stranger who came near her, and appeared apprehensive rather than aggressive, for she never bit, but only ran to the safety of her friends. All through the first two nights I suffered, intermittently, from this terrifying din screeched into my very ear-holes. She had been wont to share a bed with her late owners, and to pass most of the night upon the pillow; now she chose the foot of my bed, and, heavy and forgetful with sleep, came ambling up every half hour or so to take her accustomed position. At the discovery of a strange head on the pillow, one that seemingly never lost its dismaying novelty, she put her mouth against my ear and vented her feelings in wails and screams of abandoned anguish. I could not, perhaps, be blamed for finding this alarming; I also was recalled each time suddenly to consciousness, and to me those sounds had in the past been precursors to a bite like a leopard's.

Her call note was basically the same as Mij's, but less resonant and assertive, more plaintive and feminine. Beyond these similarities, she had a whole range of then unfamiliar expressions denoting affection, pleasure, greeting or casual conversation; notes strongly reminiscent of the human infant; most of these might, unflatteringly, fall into the category of squeals rather than chirps —unflatteringly, for they had none of the ugliness that the word connotes. Like the other otters I had owned she had a note used only when suddenly and extremely alarmed; I had heard it first from Chahala in the Tigris marshes, when the door of the reed hut was suddenly darkened by a human figure. The sound was exactly like that produced by a human being who fills his cheeks with air and expels it violently through half-closed lips. I heard it once from Mij and once from Edal.

From the very first she formed an entirely different relationship with Jimmy Watt from that which she established with me; it was, with him, a violently vocal friendship on her side, while with me, though she quickly became deeply affectionate and demonstrative, much remained tacit. Jimmy she would greet, crow over, harangue, nag, scold, caress and croon to, yell at if he disturbed her while she was sleeping, squeal with pure joy when he first appeared in the morning; with me, while she would perform the same actions, she spoke hardly a word. 'It's youth,' said Morag. 'She thinks he's another otter.' A little later other differences between the two relationships were evident, for on her daily walks she would come anywhere with me, but would not follow Jimmy if he appeared to her to be setting off in a dull or distasteful direction.

We had intended that for a full fortnight Edal should remain within the confines of the fence that enclosed the house and the pool. At first this did not seem difficult, for the pool was a new delight to her, and her moments of fretting were rare, mainly in the evenings. Then one day our attention strayed from her for a moment or two and she was gone. Where the wire joined the little shed at the north end of the house, nearest to the bridge and the route by which she had arrived with Malcolm and Paula, she had found that she could force the barrier. By the time we had made sure of her absence she had perhaps ten minutes start.

We guessed rightly the route that she had taken; when we reached Druimfiaclach she had already been there for five minutes. Morag was away, and her husband had been unable to establish *rapport* with this preoccupied creature all of whose thoughts were suddenly for the past. She lay at the top of the stairs (I have found that if there is a stairway an otter is possessed of an inalienable instinct to ascend it) and wailed piteously. She seemed pleased to see us, and greeted Jimmy with notes almost as loud as those of her distress, but she did not want to come back to Camusfeàrna. We had never put the lead on her before, but now there seemed no alternative.

The return journey took more than an hour. She would trot happily ahead for perhaps fifty yards; then she would sit down, dig in her toes, and wail. I did not realize that it would have been the easiest thing in the world to have picked her up and carried her home, with no inconvenience beyond the weight of her ponderous person, for I was still under misapprehension as to the threat contained in this item of her repertoire. As it was, the nervous strain was more exhausting than any load could have been.

A few days later she repeated this escape for the second and last time; but on that occasion Jimmy, unhampered by my conditioning to other otter language, caught her up half-way and carried her home round his neck like a lead-weighted fur collar.

Edal on the sofa.
Drawings by the author.

186

187

At the end of a fortnight there was no further danger of her straying. We had provided her with so many distractions, so many novelties—and the greatest of these was certainly constant access to running water—that she had been suborned. It was, perhaps, fortunate for us that this period of acclimatization coincided with the migration of the elvers. For these transparent morsels, who swarmed and wriggled in the rock pools below the waterfall and formed a broad snail-paced queue up the vertical rock beside the white water, she discovered a passion that obscured every other interest. Hour after hour she would pass about these pools where Mij had hunted before her, scooping and pouncing, grabbing and munching, reaching up the rock face to pluck the pilgrims as they journeyed, and from these lengthy outings she would return surfeited to play and to sleep in the kitchen as if she had known no other home.

These elvers, however, proved no small embarrassment to us, for over a period of several weeks they intermittently blocked our water supply and reduced us once again to carrying water in buckets from the burn. In our anxiety to keep Edal occupied and amused during her period of acclimatization we scooped buckets-full of the elvers and tipped them into her pool. The pool was fed by a branch of the same alkathene piping that carried our water from the top of the falls to the house; the elvers, quick to discover the only upstream exit from the pool, took up their interrupted migration with the same inflexible determination that had inspired them for the past two years, ascending the hundred-and-twenty-yard length of pipe until they reached the perforated 'rose' at the top. The perforations in the metal were, however, just too small to allow passage to their bodies, and there they stuck and died, each hole blocked by the protruding head of an elver, a pathetic and ironic end to so long and brave a journey. The 'rose' in the pool above the waterfall was accessible to us only by rope descent into the ravine; a dozen times a day we would go there and extract the dead elvers, but it was like sniping at a swarm of locusts, for behind them there were ever more of the journeying host to strangle on the very verge of liberty.

Routine is, as I have explained, of tremendous importance to animals, and as soon as we saw that Edal was settled we arranged a daily sequence that would bolster her growing security. She had her breakfast of live eels, sent, as they had been for Mij, from London, and then one or other of us took her for a two-hour walk along the shore or over the hills. During these walks she would remain far closer at hand than Mij had done, and we carried the lead not so much as a possible restraint upon her as a safeguard against attack by one of the shepherds' dogs, for Edal loved dogs, regarded them as potential playmates, and was quite unaware that many dogs in the Western Highlands are both encouraged and taught to kill otters.

On one of these morning outings with her I had a closer view of a wild otter than ever before. Edal was hunting rock-pool life on a ledge two or three yards from the sea's edge and a few feet above it; she had loitered long there among the small green crabs, butter-fish and shrimps, and my attention had wandered from her to an eagle coasting over the cliffs above me. When I turned back to the sea I saw Edal, as I thought, porpoising slowly along in the gentle waves just beyond the pool where she had been. I could have touched her with, say, the end of a salmon rod. I whistled to her and began to turn away, but as I did so the tail of my eye perceived something unfamiliar in her aspect; I looked back, and there was a wild otter staring at me with interest and surprise. I glanced down to the pool at my feet, and saw Edal, out of sight of the sea, still groping among the weed and under the flat stones. The wild otter stayed for a longer look, and then, apparently without alarm, resumed his leisurely progress southward along the edge of the rocks.

In those rock pools along the shore Edal learned to catch gobies and butter-fish; occasionally she would corner a full-grown eel in the hill streams, and little by little she discovered the speed and the predatory powers of her race. Her staple diet was of eels sent alive from London, for probably no otter can remain entirely healthy without eels, but she was also fond of ginger nuts, bacon fat, butter, and other whimsical *hors d'oeuvre* to which her upbringing by humans had conditioned her. Among local fish she disdained the saith or coal fish, tolerated lythe and trout, and would gorge herself gluttonously upon mackerel. We put her eels alive into her pool, where after early failures in the cloud of mud that her antics stirred up, she proved able to detect and capture them even in the midst of that dense smoke-screen. This is achieved, I think, by the hypersensitive tactile perception of her hands, for when in the shallow end of the pool she would appear deliberately to avert her gaze while feeling round her in the opaque water; the palms, too, are endowed with a 'non-slip' surface, composed of a number of round excrescences like the balls of fingers, which enable her to catch and hold between them an eel that would slither easily through any human grasp.

By the end of June she was swimming as an otter should, diving deep to explore dim rock ledges at the edge of the sea tangle, remaining for as much as two minutes under water, so that often only a thin track of bubbles from the imprisoned air in her fur gave guide as to her whereabouts. (This trail of bubbles, I have noticed, appears about six feet behind an otter swimming a fathom or so under-water at normal speed; never, as the eye sub-consciously expects, directly above the animal.) But though she lost her fear of depth she never felt secure in great spaces of water; she liked to see on at least one side of her the limits of the element as she swam, and when beyond this visual contact she was seized with a *horror vacui*, panicking into an infantile and frenzied dog-paddle as she raced for land.

Hence our first experiments with her in the rowing boat were not a success; the boat was to her clearly no substitute for terra firma, and in it, on deep water, she felt as insecure as if she were herself overboard—more so, in fact, for she would brave a wild rush for the shore rather than remain with us in so obvious a peril.

Edal was not the only newcomer to Camusfeàrna that summer. Years ago I had formed, at Monreith, a great collection of wild geese; after the war they represented the only major collection of rare wildfowl left in all Europe, and in 1948 they went to form the nucleus of Peter Scott's Wildfowl Trust at Slimbridge. By then, however, the commoner varieties had bred in such numbers and were so elusive to the pursuer that they were not thought worth the trouble of transporting; and the flock of full-winged greylags remained about Monreith Loch, intermittently harried for sport or as vermin to the grazing parks, semi-feral, and unwary only in the breeding season, for ten years after the collection was a thing of the past. By 1959 there were still some two or three pairs nesting at the loch, and I arranged for one brood to be hatched under a hen at Monreith and sent up to Camusfeàrna. After a long and circuitous journey by train and boat five goslings arrived, feathered but not fledged, gawky, uncouth and confiding, displaying a marked predilection for human company at variance with the traditional characteristics of their race. This paradox was pleasing to me, for like many others I had come to a fondness for wild animals and birds by way of bloodthirstiness; in my youth I had been an ardent wildfowler, and these five goslings were the direct descendants of birds I had shot and wing-tipped or otherwise lightly wounded at the morning flight years before. It had, in fact, been the keeping and taming of a few wounded greylags shot in blustering winter dawns on the salt marsh and mud-flats of Wigtown Bay that had initiated my attempt at a living collection of all the wild geese of the world, and these gabbling flat-footed five who tried so persistently to force their way into the house at Camusfeàrna were the twelfth generation, or so, in descent from the victims of my gun. Perhaps it was from some obscure part of the guilt under which, unrecognized, we labour so often, that I wanted these birds to fly free and unafraid about Camusfeàrna, wanted to hear in the dawn and the dusk the wild music of those voices that long ago used to quicken my pulse as I waited shivering in the ooze of some tidal creek with the eastern horizon aflame.

As a daily delight and as an ornament to Camusfeàrna these particular wild geese exceeded my most optimistic expectations. To begin with they were, as I have said, as yet unable to fly; only the very tips of their sprouting pinion feathers peeped out of the casing of blue blood-quill, but day-long they would stand flapping hopefully and grotesquely, lifting themselves a foot or so into the air and progressing in a series of ill co-ordinated and ungainly hops. As it had fallen to Jimmy Watt and myself, neither

of whom can swim, to teach an otter to do so, so now as the geese grew and their wing feathers became long enough for flight, but their imagination remained too small to compass the attempt, it was we who taught the wild geese to fly. Jimmy would run in front of them wildly flapping his arms in a mime of flight, until one day the goslings, performing much the same action as they hurried after him, found themselves, to their consternation, to be airborne. The immediate result was a series of most un-dignified crash landings, but in those few seconds they had found their powers; within a week they were strong and certain on the wing, and in answer to a call from the house they would come beating up the wind from the beaches of the distant islands.

At night we kept them shut up in a wire enclosure, wire floor and roof, too, as a safeguard against wildcats and foxes, and when we let them out in the morning they would rise with a great clamour and wing their way down the burn to the sea, twisting and turning in the air, 'whiffling' as wildfowlers call it, in the pure joy of their flight.

I must admit that for all their charm and beauty these five wild geese displayed, in some matters, a truly astonishing want of intellect, a plain stupidity, indeed; the very opposite of the sagacity usually ascribed to their race. Even after months of familiarity with the precincts of the house it was doubtful whether they could enter the garden gate without one or other of their number getting left behind; a goose would as often as not find himself on the wrong side of the open gate, and instead of walking round it to rejoin his companions, would concentrate upon moronic attempts to penetrate the wire that divided them from him.

More striking still was their behaviour in the pen which con-fined them at night. Every morning I would go to open the wire-netting door and release them; as soon as I appeared they would set up a gabble of greeting which reached crescendo as I lifted the barrier and they stalked out. One morning in September, being up at first light, I opened their door (which formed the whole of one side of the enclosure) some two hours earlier than the time to which they were accustomed. They greeted me as usual but did not immediately emerge, and I went back to the house think-ing that they would move only when the sun was up, and pondering afresh on the rôle of routine in animal behaviour. It was nearly three hours later, and thus long past the time when they would normally have flown down to the sea, that I caught sight of them from the kitchen window. They were still inside the pen, chattering irritably, and walking up and down in front of the open door as if some invisible barrier separated them from the grass outside. Deciding that they could only be liberated by some symbolic gesture, I went out to them exactly as if we had not met that morning; I closed the door and then re-opened it with a flourish, talking to them the while as I was wont. With profound relief apparent, one would have said, in their every action, they came trooping out at my heels and almost at once took wing for the shore.

From the last days of May until early September the summer, that year, took leave of absence; while England panted in equatorial heat and the coast roads from London were jammed by twenty-mile queues of motionless cars, Camusfeàrna saw only sick gleams of sunshine between the ravings of gale and rain; the burn came down in roaring spate, and the sea was restless and petulant under the unceasing winds. The bigger dinghy dragged her moorings and stove a plank, and there were few days when the little flat-bottomed pram could take the sea without peril. Because of this, and because, perhaps, I welcomed Edal's fear of the open sea as a factor in favour of her safety, it was not until the first of September that we renewed experiments with her in the boats.

She had gained much confidence meanwhile, both in us and in her proper element, and she gambolled round us in the warm sunshine as we dragged the pram across the sand into a still blue sea that reflected the sky without so much as a ripple. The geese, ever companionable and anxious to share activity, followed us in a chuckling procession down the beach, and the whole strange convoy set off from the tide's edge together; Edal shooting through the clear, bright sea, grabbing and clasping the oar blades or bouncing inboard with a flurry of aerated water, the geese paddling along a few yards astern with mildly disapproving eyes behind their orange bills. We rowed for a mile down the coast-line, with the glorious ochres and oranges of tide-bared weed as a foreground to the heather, reddening bracken, and the blue distances of mountain heights. All the magic of Camusfeàrna was fixed in that morning; the vivid lightning streak of an otter below water; the wheeling, silver-shouldered flight of the geese as they passed to alight ahead of us; the long, lifting, blue swell of the sea among the skerries and the sea tangle; the little rivers of froth and crystal that spilled back from the rocks as each smooth wave sucked back and left them bare.

Edal, finding herself from time to time swimming above an apparently bottomless abyss, would still panic suddenly and rush for the boat in a racing dog-paddle, her head above water and not daring to look down; her instinctive memories, it seemed, alternated between those of the dim mysterious depths and forests of waving weed, and the security of the hearth rug, lead, and reassuring human hands. So she would turn suddenly for the boat (of which she had now lost all fear and felt to be as safe as the dry land), a small anxious face above furiously striking forefeet, cleaving the surface with a frothing arrow of wave, and leap aboard with her skin-load of water. Then she would poise herself on the gunwale, webbed hind feet gripping tensely, head submerged, peering down on the knife edge between sea and terra firma, between the desire for submarine exploration and the fear of desertion in the deep unknown. Sometimes she would slide, soundlessly and almost without ripple, into deep water, only to panic as soon as she had submerged and strike out again frantically for the boat. Yet in the moments when her confidence had not yet deserted her, when the slim torpedo of her form glided deep below the boat's side, weaving over the white sand between tall, softly-waving trees of bright weed, or darting in sudden swift pursuit of some prey invisible from above, it seemed as if the clock had been set back and it was Mijbil who followed the dinghy through the shining water.

After the first of these paradise days among the islands the geese failed for the first time to return at nightfall. In the morning I called for them, but there was no greeting chorus in reply. It was as yet early for them to have felt any migratory instinct, which I thought would in any case have probably been extinguished by some generations of static forebears, and when I had seen no sign of them by the afternoon I feared that they had wandered too far and fallen prey to some tourist with a .22 rifle. I had, indeed, given up all hope of them when in the early evening I landed with Edal upon one of the white-sand beaches of the islands, drawn there by the desire to make the acquaintance of some visitors who had landed from a sailing dinghy. I was talking to them when I saw, half a mile or so to the northward, the long unhurried beat of goose wings against the sky, and recognized, with an absurd surge of joy, my missing greylags. I called to them as they made to pass high overhead in the sunshine, and they checked in mid air and came spiralling down in steep, vibrant descent, to alight with a flurry of pinions on the sand at our feet.

It never ceased to give me delight, this power to summon wild geese from the heavens as they passed, seemingly steady as a constellation upon their course, or to call to them from the house when the sun was dipping behind the hills of Skye, to hear far off their answering clangour, and see the silhouette of their wings beating in from the sea against the sunset sky. I found more enjoyment in that brood of humble greylags than ever I had in the great collection of exotic wildfowl of which their ancestors had been the discarded dregs, the lees, not worth removal; more pleasure, perhaps, in their peaceful, undemanding co-existence than had any medieval nobleman in the hawk who at his bidding rose to take the wild duck as they flew or hurl the heron from the sky.

Though the greylags gave little trouble and much reward, they produced on occasion, as do all creatures for whom one is responsible, moments of acute anxiety. The worst of these was the sight of one of their number, out of my reach, doing its utmost to swallow a fish hook. Edal, as I have said, was fed upon live eels sent from London; this was a costly procedure, and as she grew and her consumption of eels rose beyond the original order for six pounds a week, I had begun experiments to supply her from the Camusfeàrna burn, in which eels abounded. But despite much advice I had failed signally to devise a satisfactory eel trap, and one afternoon we set a number of short lines from the bridge, baited with worms. This proved effective, and we had several eels in a few hours, but I had forgotten the geese. They were not often at the bridge, and I had not thought, in any case, that they would be inquisitive enough to investigate the almost invisible lines. Some two hours later, nevertheless, they chose perversely to fly in there from the sea, and by the time that I saw them one had a foot-length of trout cast dangling from its bill. At the end of the cast was the hook, a small hook taken from a stripped trout fly, and the goose, unaware of danger, was trying hard to swallow what remained. The fineness of the cast was all that impeded the intention, but while I watched in an agony of suspense another two or three inches disappeared from view. The other geese gathered round my feet, but this one, intent upon its personal problem, kept obstinately to the centre of the pool, while the hook, in response to the gobbling movements of the bill, mounted steadily higher. In the nick of time we lured it to the bank with an offer of food, and when I gripped the cast and pulled I found myself hauling it out hand over hand, for the bird had some five feet of line in its crop. The incident put a temporary full stop to my efforts to supply Edal with eels from the burn.

For the same reason the geese became an embarrassment, too, to fishing expeditions at sea; when they did not actually accompany the boat out from the beach they would discern it from afar, long after we thought to have eluded their pursuit; they would come winging out over the waves and alight, gabbling, alongside, pressing in close round the darrow line, fascinated by the

fish-hooks and the dancing blue-and-silver glitter of fish hauled in over the gunwale, so that often it became necessary to control a darrow-full of mackerel with one hand and fend the geese from danger with the other. It was at such moment that I understood how difficult life would be if all wild animals and birds were unafraid of man; how complicated the every-day business of living must have become to St. Francis.

14

THE HOUSE had been much transformed since Edal's arrival. While there had been no otter at Camusfeàrna I had concentrated upon improving the décor and comfort of the rooms; now that the whole premises were once more, as it were, in a state of siege this aspect had perforce to be abandoned for more practical considerations. Every table and shelf had somehow to be raised above the range of Edal's agile inquisition; every hanging object upon the walls moved upward like the population of a flooded town seeking sanctuary upon the rooftops. No longer could there be a paper-table at the end of the sofa, for this recently constructed innovation she appropriated for her own on the first day, tearing and crumpling the effete reading matter until it formed a bed suited to her exacting taste. There she lay upon her back and slept, her head pillowed across a headline describing traffic jams on the roads out of London.

It was exceedingly difficult to elevate every vulnerable object above her reach, for by standing on tiptoe she could already achieve three foot six inches. When wet she would pull down a towel, or several towels, upon which to dry herself; when bored she would possess herself of any object that caught her wayward fancy, and, deeply absorbed, set about its systematic disintegration. These moods would come and go; there were days when she was as sedate as a lap dog, but there were days, too, when there simply was not room enough on the walls for the fugitives from her depredations. By nature of its surroundings Camusfeàrna is heavily-stocked with rubber boots, both Wellingtons and sea-boots; many of these have over a period of years been patched with red-rubber discs, and Edal early found a fiendish delight in tearing these off and enlarging the holes they hid.

Thus the rooms to which she had access acquired the look of country-house parks whose trees display the 'browsing line' so much deplored by late eighteenth-century writers on landscape gardening. From the height above ground to which the trees were branchless it was, in those parks, possible to deduce whether the owner kept fallow deer, cattle, or horses, and by much the same process I was able to compare the relative sizes of Edal and Mij. If there was any doubt at first, at the end of her first month with me she was certainly a much larger creature, and yet she was still a full six months younger than he had been when he was killed. Her growth was almost visible. In May Malcolm Macdonald had estimated that she was some forty-two inches long and weighed twenty-five pounds; by August she was close on fifty inches, and I estimated her weight as not far short of forty pounds. She was then a year old, and since she had not yet come into season it was clear that her growth was far from complete. In equatorial America there are otters the size of seals; if they have ever been domesticated the rooms of their owners must present a most curious appearance.

Because of the limitations of wall space in the kitchen-living-room it was not advisable to leave Edal quite alone there for long periods. She was more accommodating in this matter of being left alone than Mij had been, and if she had been exercised and fed she was content for five hours or more. When we went by boat to the village or over to Skye we would leave her shut into a room given up entirely to her, the unfurnished room over the kitchen, that had served the same purpose in Mij's day. Here she had her bed, made from a motor tyre covered with rugs; her lavatory in a corner, composed of newspapers laid on American cloth (to this somewhat remote convenience she would dutifully ascend from the kitchen whenever necessary); a host of miscellaneous toys; and dishes of water. This room had one great disadvantage: it had a single-plank floor and it was directly above the living-room. Though her water bowls were of the non-upsettable variety made for dogs, they were far from non-upsettable to her, for having tried and failed to tip them by leverage she would simply pick them up in both hands and over-turn them; and the ceiling was, as I have indicated, far from water-proof. In the early days, too, her marksmanship at her lavatory was none too accurate, and this was unfortunately situated at a point roughly above the chair where any casual guest would normally sit.

Water multiplies its value to an otter as soon as it is falling or otherwise on the move, and Edal discovered that having over-turned her bowl upstairs it was possible to scamper down to the kitchen and receive the double dividend of the drops falling through the ceiling; I have seen her on the kitchen floor, head up and mouth wide open, catching every drip as it pattered down from above.

It was a source of great disappointment to Edal that the few dogs she was allowed to meet fell far short of her standards as playmates. In general their attitude towards her reminded me of nothing so much as the colour-bar, and she clearly felt hurt and chagrined at their failure to accept her as one of themselves. With few exceptions they growled, barked, and snarled at her over-tures. The first, a sedate Golden Labrador bitch, sat in front of the fire with her back turned to Edal in a most marked manner; every now and again Edal, discouraged from more direct approach by an unequivocal snap, would tentatively stretch out one of her monkey-like hands and touch the unresponsive yellow rump, making, the while, little plaintive, yearning whines in the back of her throat. She was plainly puzzled by her failure to establish friendly relations, for she was unused to rebuff.

Two dogs only achieved with her a temporary *bonhomie*, but both, after a short time, found her personality too overpowering. A peculiarly zany, yellow-eyed pointer bitch, brought over by James Robertson Justice, entered to begin with into the true spirit that Edal required of her playmates, racing round and round in dazzling circles while Edal displayed remarkable judgment in the matter of short cuts—too remarkable for the pointer, who ended upon her back in the burn while Edal mocked her from the bank. This incident produced a coolness that their relationship did not survive; the pointer became wary and then frankly hostile. When I expostulated at this deplorable lack of stamina her owner replied, 'Well, she never thought she was going to be called upon to make sport for an otter, least of all one called Crumpet.' (Like most curious pets Edal had, since her arrival at Camusfeàrna, acquired a variety of alternative names, among which this was perhaps one of the least regrettable.)

Eric Linklater introduced a great rangy English Setter, a gorgeous beast named Tops'l, and he, too, was at first prepared to chance his arm playing with an otter, this time on the sand; but, like the pointer, he found his ability to make rings round her set at nought by her unerring eye for radii. Thus consistently outwitted, he took refuge in hysterical barking, and Edal took refuge in the sea. I still hope some time to find a dog who will play with her as Priscilla did in Africa.

202

The otter and the five greylag geese were the resident familiars of Camusfeàrna, though during the course of the summer there were other, more transient visitors; a young Slavonian Grebe that from all the multitudinous waters of that landscape chose to alight upon the tiny pool that we had dug behind the house for Edal, and found the surrounding wire-netting too high to permit take-off; a miserable blind young vole dropped by its parent as she carried it in torrential rain from the suddenly-flooded ditches of forestry drainage, and which survived for four days fed from a laborious replica of a mouse's teat; a wounded and scarcely fledged herring gull, picked up near to the house, dying in deluge and gale, who recovered to develop both flight and a degree of dependence upon household scraps; and a land rail, that arrived from the village in a cardboard box on the back of whose label was written, 'What bird is this, and is it usually found perched by the fire-side?' It had, inexplicably, been discovered squatting by the empty hearth when the householder came down in the morning. It was a great surprise to me, this bird of which a more usual view is in short flimsy flight low over the rushes of some snipe bog, the most unambitious of aerial enterprises, ending abruptly in a landing that, though invisible, one feels can only be ungraceful and inept. A thoroughly undistinguished bird, one would say, nondescript in plumage, gauche in action, and in habits retiring to the point of non-entity. Yet the specimen in the cardboard box, thus forced as it were into propinquity and social contact with mankind, revealed itself as dapper, even dressy, in personal appearance, with irascible ruby-red eyes and an aggres-sive, choleric temperament. He flew like a fighting cock at any hand that approached him, and the deceptively slender red bill had a grip like a pair of pliers. He clearly resented every detail of his ignominious captivity, but he had arrived in the evening and I did not want to set him free until I was sure that he was uninjured; he spent the night in my bedroom, whose floor was for the occasion littered with earthworms and other unsavoury offerings; either in pursuit of these or in simple self-assertion he stamped about all night making, as the occupant of the room beneath put it, a noise like a mouse in hob-nailed boots. Daylight showed him to be sound in wind and limb, and he resumed anonymity in a larger landscape.

Finally, producing a more lasting impression, came a wildcat kitten. Late one afternoon we had discovered that the Calor-gas cylinder (an innovation that year) was almost exhausted, and we decided to take the boat up at once to the village five miles away. It was a blue-and-gold September afternoon, with the sea between the islands as smooth as the face of a cut and polished stone. The tide was ebbing and the tops of the sea tangle showing between the skerries, so that had we not been pressed for time before the village shop would close we should have passed outside the lighthouse point; now the possible saving of ten minutes seemed a worthy gamble against the danger of running aground, and we decided to try the channel between the lighthouse island and its neighbour. I was at the tiller, and Jimmy Watt was kneeling in the bows, directing me between the rocks. Suddenly he called my attention excitedly to something at the surface on our port bow.

There, fifteen yards away, was a half-grown wildcat kitten, swimming uncertainly in the direction of the farther island. (I have since learned that it is no rarity for wildcats to take to the water, even when they are not pursued, but at the moment it seemed as strange as would a fish progressing over land.) The cat was in about two fathoms of water, and swam slowly and very high, so that the whole back and tail were above water and dry. I tried to turn towards it, but at that precise moment the out-board engine bracket, which in our hurry to set off had not been tightened securely on the transom, came adrift on one side and left me without steering. To our amazement the cat then appeared to turn towards the boat as if towards rescue, and by forcing the engine into the water with one hand I was able to bring the bows alongside it. I had never handled a living wildcat, and I thought the least that Jimmy was in for was a bad scratching, but there was not so much as a snarl as he grasped it round the body, lifted it from the sea, and dumped it into a wicker hamper. It was difficult to associate this meek, fluffy, lost kitten with the un-tameable ferocity of all reports, and I thought that here was the opportunity to test the rumours at first hand. But it was difficult to see how Camusfeàrna could contain with any placidity both a wildcat and an otter, and my thoughts turned to Morag; she, I thought, would welcome this ghost of her childhood days, for long ago she had kept, and mourned the loss of, a hybrid with a wildcat sire. She was at that time housekeeping, during the daylight hours, for the lodge by the river four miles up the coast, so we abandoned our idea of replenishing the Calor-gas supplies and headed for the river. Morag, however, had already left by the mail Land Rover for Driumfiaclach; at the lodge we were lent a car, and continued to her home by road. The calm of the cat within the hamper had by now given place to a low but almost continual growl, a menacing sound that suggested a curbed ferocity hardly held in rein.

When I learned that Morag felt herself too cramped by household duties to commit herself to the care of a wildcat, I should, no doubt, have released it, but despite all that I had heard and read of the untameable nature of wildcats I had met no one who could personally contribute to the picture; I knew, too, that it was very rare to capture an undamaged kitten, and I felt that an opportunity to test the validity of the myth was not to be thrown away. I returned to the lodge, and from there telephoned to Dr. Maurice Burton, a zoologist who at his home in Surrey keeps and observes a great variety of wild creatures, and who had in the course of a lifetime devoted to the study of animal behaviour acquired experience of most British fauna. Curiously, however, he proved never to have kept a wildcat, and knew no one who had ever tried to tame one, though he did know someone whose lifelong ambition it had been to acquire a healthy kitten for the experiment. He proposed telephoning to this friend, who would in turn telephone to me during the next half hour, and in due course I spoke to Mr. William Kingham, who was prepared to leave London by car at dawn the next morning to collect the cat. It was then Friday evening; he expected to complete the seven-hundred-mile journey by Sunday morning.

I carried the now distinctly vocal hamper back by boat to Camusfeàrna. There was only one way of bridging the next thirty-six hours: to evacuate my bedroom in favour of the kitten and to sleep in the kitchen. This I did with some reluctance, not because I envisaged the shambles to which my room would be reduced, but because it had been but three nights before that I had returned to it after the departure of my last guest.

It was already dark when we beached the boat below the house, and there was no means of obtaining any suitable food for a wild-cat that night. I left the hamper open in my bedroom beside a saucer of tinned milk and some sea-trout roes. As an afterthought I blocked the chimney with a screwed-up ball of wire-netting.

In the morning, after a far from novel night in a sleeping-bag by the kitchen fire, a cursory inspection of the bedroom discovered no cat. One of the trout roes and all the milk had disappeared, and there was an odoriferous mess in the centre of my bed, but of the perpetrator of this outrage there was no sign whatever. Just so, I remember, would we as children incarcerate hedgehogs in rooms that would not have offered exit to a mouse and yet find on awakening, eager and unwashed, not so much as a single spine to tell us that it had not been a dream. I have since suspected the adult world of some nocturnal interference in the matter, but in those days we were both fatalistic and ingenuous.

A more detailed examination revealed the cat, in the chimney. It had pulled out the inadequate cork of wire mesh, and was ensconced, owl-like, on a ledge some two feet above and to one side of the grate. My first tentative fumblings drove it up higher into the dim funnel, into regions accessible only to weapons of remote control such as chimney brushes.

I was distressed by this, for recapture was clearly necessary, and equally clearly would be a traumatic experience for the subject of an experiment in domestication. But there was no alternative, and Jimmy Watt, armed with a long string and a weight, scaled the roof while I waited, heavily-gloved, to grasp the kitten when it should descend within range.

The gloves proved, in fact, to be encouragingly unnecessary; there was a certain amount of snarling and spitting, but no retaliation whatsoever. Liberated, the cat made one bound for the darkest corner of the room, and remained there, eyes glowing dully, while I made the chimney impregnable.

Sunday morning came and there was devastation in every corner of my bedroom, but there was no sign of any relief party from the south. During the night, it seemed, my captive had enjoyed the greatest of high spirits; it had concentrated not upon escape but destruction, tearing up letters, playing ball with ink-bottles, ascending with airy grace to remote shelves beyond the wildest dreams of any otter. It had dined well upon the carcase of an oyster-catcher, of which nothing but the wing feathers and the bill remained. The insult on the centre of the bed had been repeated, louder and clearer, so to speak, than before. The cat had taken up daylight quarters in a peat creel, a wicker pannier designed to be carried by a pony, that we had found washed up on the beach, and which now hung on the wall as a wastepaper basket beyond the reach of otters.

The necessity for shooting birds locally in order to feed this creature worried me. Many of the birds in the immediate vicinity of Camusfeàrna were tamer, more trusting, than in areas where someone or other was constantly on the prowl with a gun; not only was I reluctant to disturb this tranquillity, but I felt, as I set out from the house with a loaded weapon, like a deliberate traitor to the small sanctuary that I had long respected. The situation was made no easier for me by the geese, who insisted on accompanying me, sometimes on foot, sometimes locating me from afar and flying in to join me as I crouched, camouflaged, on the rock of some outlying skerry; by them I was embarrassed, obscurely ashamed that they should witness this predatory side to my nature. I found myself, as I crouched there in the salt wind and spray, repeating a childish little litany: 'I am only doing this so that the kitten may live'; this, by some absentminded transposition, reshaped itself into the words and tune of a forgotten hymn 'He died that we might live'; and then I realized that my subconscious mind had jumped a gap at which my intellect had jibbed—for after all Christians do eat the body and blood of their God.

So, with distaste, I kept the wildcat supplied with birds that I would rather have seen alive: a turnstone, a shag, an oystercatcher, and a curlew, and my unwilling guest consumed them all with relish and went on defecating squarely in the middle of my bed. I put a box of earth on the floor, but though it was much dug by morning and smelled strongly of ammonia the bed remained the major receptacle.

On the Monday a telegram arrived explaining that Mr. Kingham had reached Glasgow a day earlier, only to be overtaken by sickness that had compelled him to turn back. Unaware that the number from which I had spoken to him was five miles by sea, he asked me to telephone to him in Surrey that evening.

The relief that I had hourly awaited being thus indefinitely postponed, I set off again for the village with a faltering outboard motor which completed the northward but not the return journey. By intermittent use of the oars I got home late at night, with the promise of an immediate telegram about the future of the wildcat.

There were further delays and misunderstandings, but a week after the original capture an emissary arrived at the railhead twelve miles north by sea, and dispatched a hired launch to Camusfeàrna. He did not accompany it himself; I had assumed that he would arrive to stay for the night and receive such information as I could give him about the wildcat's habits, so that I was quite unprepared for boxing the animal at once with the launch waiting outside on an ebb tide. However, though the human escort was absent he had sent a stout and commodious crate filled with straw, at the back of which lay a plump un-plucked pullet.

To the cat this third and necessarily hurried capture was still further trauma. He—for excremental reasons I vaguely supposed it to be a male—was crouched on a high shelf in the shadow of my typewriter (already knocked down and smashed by the otter), and the first advance of a gloved hand produced a tigerish and highly intimidating snarl of warning. On the second attempt he bounded from the shelf to a table in the window and crouched there growling with his back to the glass.

At this point Jimmy, who had been out in the boat fishing for mackerel when the launch came, arrived and demanded to take control. He put on the gloves and entered the arena with all the confidence of inexperience. At his first near approach the cat became transformed; almost, I had said, transfigured. The last trace of resemblance to a fluffy domestic Persian kitten vanished utterly; in its place was a noble, savage wild animal at bay before its ancestral enemy. Laying his ears not back but downward from the broad flat skull, so that the very tips and the tufts of hair that grew from within them were all that turned upward, baring every fang and gum in his head so that the yellow eyes became slits of rage and hate, swelling his ringed tail to twice its previous girth, he reared himself back against the glass of the window pane. But while one paw was lifted high with extended talons, the other still rested on the table, for the forelegs seemed to have elongated like telescopes; those velvet limbs had in an instant changed from instruments of locomotion into long-reaching weapons to rake and to slash. As an image of primordial ferocity

I had seen nothing to equal it; it was splendid, it was magnificent, but it was war.

Jimmy, as yet accustomed only to handling creatures whose bluff was easily called, was undismayed by this display of *fuchtbarkeit*, but retired after an instant with a bite clean through glove and thumb-nail.

It seemed as if deadlock had been reached, until it occurred to us that we could as it were bottle the cat between the open end of the crate and the window glass; this manoeuvre was instantly successful, and he bolted to the dim interior behind the straw and was silent. That was the last that I saw of him; it is, however, not improbable that we shall meet again, for his new owner undertook that if the cat followed the pattern of legend and proved untameable it should be returned to Camusfeàrna and freed where wildcats enjoy the privilege of protection.

It is October, and I have been for six unbroken months at Camusfeàrna. The stags are roaring on the slopes of Skye across the Sound, and yesterday the wild swans passed flying southwards low over a lead-grey sea. The ring of tide-wrack round the bay is piled with fallen leaves borne down the burn, and before a chill sea wind they are blown racing and scurrying up the sands. The summer, with its wild roses and smooth blue seas lapping white island beaches, is over; the flower of the heather is dead and the scarlet rowan berries fallen. Beyond are the brief twilit days of winter, when the waterfall will thunder white over flat rocks whose surface was hot to bare feet under summer suns, and the cold, salt-wet wind will rattle the windows and moan in the chimney. This year I shall not be there to see and hear these things; home is for me as yet a fortress from which to essay raid and foray, an embattled position behind whose walls one may retire to lick new wounds and plan fresh journeys to farther horizons. Yet while there is time there is the certainty of return.

Camusfeàrna
October 1959

Thank you, my friendly daemon, close to me as my shadow
For the mealy buttercup days in the ancient meadow,
For the days of my 'teens, the sluice of hearing and seeing,
The days of topspin drives and physical well-being.

Thank you, my friend, shorter by a head, more placid
Than me your protégé whose ways are not so lucid,
My animal angel sure of touch and humour
With face still tanned from some primeval summer.

Thanks for your sensual poise, your gay assurance,
Who skating on the lovely wafers of appearance
Have held my hand, put vetoes upon my reason,
Sent me to look for berries in the proper season.

Some day you will leave me or, at best, less often
I shall sense your presence when eyes and nostrils open,
Less often find your burgling fingers ready
To pick the locks when mine are too unsteady.

Thank you for the times of contact, for the glamour
Of pleasure sold by the clock and under the hammer,
Thank you for bidding for me, for breaking the cordon
Of spies and sentries round the unravished garden.

And thank you for the abandon of your giving,
For seeing in the dark, for making this life worth living.